Paths to
Discovery

Paths to Discovery

Autobiographies from Chicanas with Careers in Science, Mathematics, and Engineering

Norma E. Cantú, Editor

With an Introduction by
Aída Hurtado

CSRC Director: Chon A. Noriega
Senior Editor: Rebecca Frazier
Manuscript Editor: Michelle Nordon
Design and Production: William Morosi

UCLA Chicano Studies Research Center
193 Haines Hall
Los Angeles, California, USA 90095-1544
press@chicano.ucla.edu
www.chicano.ucla.edu

Library of Congress Cataloging-in-Publication Data

Paths to discovery : autobiographies from chicanas with careers in science, mathematics, and engineering / Norma E. Cantú, editor ; with an introduction by Aída Hurtado. -- 1st ed.
    p. cm.
  Includes bibliographical references and index.
  ISBN 978-0-89551-119-5 (paper edition : alk. paper)
  1. Women scientists--United States--Biography. 2. Women scientists--Mexico--Biography. 3. Hispanic American scientists--Biography. 4. Scientists--United States--Biography. 5. Scientists--Mexico--Biography. 6. Women engineers--United States--Biography. 7. Women engineers--Mexico--Biography. 8. Hispanic American engineers--Biography. 9. Engineers--United States--Biography. 10. Engineers--Mexico--Biography. I. Cantú, Norma Elia, 1947-
  Q141.P3746 2008
  509.2'273--dc22
  [B]
                        2007047071

♾ The paper used in this publication meets the minimum requirements of the American National Standard for Information Sciences—Permanence of Paper for Printed Library Materials, ANSI Z39-48-1994.

We dedicate this book to all future Latina scientists, mathematicians, and engineers who question, who aspire, and who seek to live a life of the mind.

A todas las mujeres del pasado y las del futuro.

CONTENTS

Part III. Pasos con Veredas

ACKNOWLEDGMENTS Y GRACIAS

We would like to thank everyone involved in the making of *Paths to Discovery: Autobiographies from Chicanas with Careers in Science, Mathematics, and Engineering,* a new version of *Flor y Ciencia: Chicanas in Mathematics, Science and Engineering* (published in 2006). We want to acknowledge the help of Cynthia Eckstein at the National Science Foundation (NSF), for facilitating the NSF Grant # BES-0339201, and the funding that made possible our initial gathering at the Mujeres Activas en Letras y Cambio Social (MALCS) annual meeting in San Antonio, Texas. Our heartfelt gratitude to our many colleagues, friends, and families who read our pieces and offered comments and suggestions for our stories, or who helped with scanning or securing the photographs. Finally, we thank and laud the wonderful editorial staff at the Chicano Studies Research Center (CSRC) at the University of California, Los Angeles, especially Wendy Belcher, Rebecca Frazier, Michelle Nordon, Dianne Woo, and the CSRC director, Chon A. Noriega, for their support and for seeing the merits of publishing our stories.

I hesitated when Elvia Niebla, a scientist working at the time as national coordinator for the U.S. Department of Agriculture's Forest Service Global Change Research Program, approached me about applying to the National Science Foundation (NSF) for a grant to invite young Chicana graduate students in science, engineering, and mathematics to the annual gathering of the Mujeres Activas en Letras y Cambio Social (MALCS). As a humanities person, I was more familiar with the National Endowment for the Humanities and the National Endowment for the Arts, and knew very little about the workings of the NSF. Besides, as the chair of the local arrangements committee for the conference/institute, I had precious little time to devote to yet another aspect of the three-day event. Why would I want to make more work for myself? The answer was obvious: because I knew how important it was to work across our disciplinary borders, and because our *hermanas* in the sciences had not often joined us in the social sciences and in the humanities. The grant would also fulfill one of the goals of MALCS, namely, to mentor Chicana graduate students. We titled our project *"Adelante!"* for we believed it could help Chicanas advance in fields where they had been traditionally absent.

That August of 2003, as the conference came to an end and the twenty-seven young participants expressed their joy and gratitude for having met so many Mexican American scientists and mathematicians, I knew our work was not over. We asked for an extension for *"Adelante!"* from the NSF and proceeded to the next phase of the project, a phase that was added as an afterthought, but one that I felt was a perfect, and necessary, follow-up. I had been privileged to work on the anthology *Telling to Live: Latina Feminist Testimonios*, and one of our goals with that project was to have other groups of women follow our lead and also tell their stories. With *"Adelante!"* came an excellent opportunity to realize those goals, for a new group of women to give their narratives and offer them to other Latinas in higher education. And so, out of *"Adelante!"* came *Flor y Ciencia: Chicanas in Mathematics, Science and Engineering*, a book rooted in our desire to mentor young women and to tell the stories of those who have been down the path before them, those we call the trailblazers, *las abrecaminos*, those who have survived the challenges of being Chicanas in the traditionally male and white disciplines of mathematics, science, and engineering. This book is a revision of *Flor y Ciencia*; I changed the title to *Paths to Discovery: Autobiographies from Chicanas with Careers in Science, Mathematics, and Engineering*, and added one more author, whose voice joins the nine other Chicanas with her story.

The original book project materialized as we gathered in August 2004, a year after that initial MALCS conference, once again in San Antonio, to articulate what we wanted the book to be. Subsequent meetings followed. All of these gatherings were full of joy and laughter; they also provided support and a space to air our differences and share our views on our positions within the various professional sectors we occupy. While most of us are professors in university settings, this is not so for all. Among us are community college and public school teachers, as well as government and civil service workers. We are a geographically diverse group, and although mostly over fifty, we are at various stages of our careers, including the stage of anticipating retirement. But all of the contributing writers are devoted to their community and to promoting Chicanas in science, math, and engineering.

Over the past few years, I have become aware of two recurring themes of our legacy: the power of *testimonio* writing, and the great need to recruit those who will succeed us. Indeed, those who belong to our generation of *abrecaminos*, those pathmakers who were the "first" in a myriad of careers, are either passing on or retiring from academic work. Who will take our places in the classrooms and laboratories? Who will become the next generation of leaders present at the table when decisions are being made, and who will ensure that Latinas are not absent or erased from the script? While research on the status of Latinos/as in the sciences shows an increase in the number of graduate students, education statistics tell of an alarming number of dropouts from high school and college, not to mention the number of Latino students who arrive in the college classroom with dreams of becoming researchers, medical doctors, or engineers, only to find that they are ill prepared for the rigors of academics. Poor preparation, lack of resources, and an inhospitable environment all contribute to the change in majors that frequently occurs shortly after the first year in college.

Despite demographic growth, Latinos/as continue to be underrepresented in what are traditionally referred to as STEM fields (science, technology, engineering, and mathematics); according to the National Center for Education Statistics, they make up only 3 percent of the nation's scientists and engineers. In a similar effort to ours and in an attempt to encourage Latina/os to pursue engineering careers, Edna Gravenhorst published *¡Ay, Mija! Why Do You Want to Be an Engineer?* in 2006, and, more recently, a second book, *¡Ay, Mijo! Why Do You Want to Be an Engineer?* In *Paths to Discovery*, we have added a fact sheet compiled by Deborah Santiago of the Excelencia in Education organization to demonstrate the dire state of affairs.

With these obstacles in mind, our book offers young women a road map for entering the sciences, territory that has already been traveled by our contributors. Their stories, not unlike those in *Telling to Live*, are *testimonios* that tell of arriving at college poorly prepared academically and of being faced with enormous personal obstacles. But they also tell of mentors who encouraged, who offered support, and who made a difference. Indeed, the *testimonios* in *Paths to Discovery* testify to the indomitable will of these women to overcome, to resist, to succeed.

We believe that the publication of *Paths to Discovery* is necessary at this point for many reasons. For example, when *Flor y Ciencia* was published in 2006, we realized that we needed to publish a much larger run to meet the demands of educators and students in the STEM fields. As I worked to revise and prepare this new manuscript, I felt that I was following Gloria Anzaldúa's urging to "do work that matters." We are at a critical point as the earlier generation of science professors retires and the pipeline is not much healthier than it was thirty years ago. We must continue the task of encouraging and preparing young Chicanas to enter the fields of mathematics, science, and engineering.

In the tradition of *testimonio*, rooted as it is in Latin American resistance literature, these stories inspire and encourage, urge and demand that these conditions change for Chicanas; they are an indictment of systems that have traditionally denied access to and marginalized Chicanas who aspire to enter these fields. How our schools have shortchanged Chicanas who would have been scientists, mathematicians, and engineers, I cannot imagine. But through these stories that tell of those who survived and pursued their dream in spite of such conditions, we come to understand the factors that made it possible to succeed, to walk a path that few have walked—the helping hand, the family support, the encouraging teacher, and most of all the *ganas*, the desire to pursue that dream. With this in mind, I hope that the stories I have gathered here will provide a road map, and that they will tell young Chicanas that others have done it and so can they. After all, we must do whatever it takes to make the path easier for those who follow it.

It has been a privilege and an honor to work with these outstanding women, to hear their stories, and to get to know them and their passion for their fields of work and study. To them I say *gracias* for allowing me this opportunity. To you, the reader, I say "Enjoy!" and take heart from these stories that prove *que sí se puede*!

Norma E. Cantú
San Antonio, Tejas
August 2007

Un Cuadro–
A Framing

Aída Hurtado

Success in this society is often attributed to individual perseverance and will. The Horatio Alger story is alive and well in the U.S. imagination as a way to explain our acceptance of meritocracy. The fields of mathematics and natural sciences are fertile grounds for exploring the myth of individual success and how it may mask other possible explanations for why individuals outside the mainstream flourish and make impressive contributions to their field's knowledge base.

Chicana scientists, given their small numbers and relative obscurity, are often thought of as individuals of extraordinary strength who have succeeded against all odds. In the autobiographical essays that follow in this book, however, the stories are much more complicated and nuanced. If there is one overarching similarity among them, it is that individual perseverance alone is not sufficient to succeed in male-dominated fields. Instead, what the stories uncover is a web of caring and support that propelled these Chicanas—predominantly working class, first generation in college, of Color, and women—into spheres previously uninhabited by people like them. Noting their embeddedness in social relations, rather than simply focusing on their achievements as individuals, reveals a much more complex and textured explanation for their success. So what can be gleaned from these Chicana scientists' narratives of their life trajectories that will help guide the next generation of pioneers in such fields as mathematics, chemistry, and biology? The themes of their childhoods and adult lives hold valuable lessons worthy of closer examination.

Master Narratives of Success

To better understand the lives of the contributors to this book, it is necessary to look beyond "master narratives" of educational success. Several of the ten contributors were the first in their families to graduate from high school, much less finish college and obtain advanced degrees in demanding fields in the academy. Furthermore, six of the contributors are tenured in some of the most prestigious institutions of higher education in the world. Mary Romero and Abigail Stewart (1999) would readily agree that the narratives in this volume contribute to the increasing number of "women's untold stories" that either purposely or inadvertently negate the master narratives of achievement. Romero and Stewart discuss master narratives as the template by which individuals make sense of their lives, as well as the lives of those around them: "Our rich and complex culture offers many different narratives to women (and to men), as tools for understanding themselves and others. These stories operate as 'master narratives' when they subsume many differences and contradictions and restrict and contain people, by supporting a power structure in which gender, class, race/ethnicity, sexuality, and ability all define who matters and how" (xiv).

Master narratives are also used to reinscribe power among groups such that "the dominant group creates its own stories, as well.... The stories or narratives told by the ingroup remind it of its identity in relation to outgroups, and provide it with a form of shared reality in which its own superior position is seen as natural" (Delgado 1995, 64). Master narratives serve as frameworks to create social policy, to market salable media, and to evaluate evidence in law proceedings, among many other functions (Romero and Stewart 1999). The power of master narratives lies in their apparent normality—"that's just the way things are"—and the internalization of such narratives into the "common sense" of our everyday lives. As Romero and Stewart elaborate, "Master narratives are stories that are so familiar they seem inevitable and obvious in their meaning, even when they happen to us. Master narratives are the stories we were taught and teach ourselves about who does what and why. They are often elaborated, plot-filled stereotypes that tell us not only what someone is like but also where they've come from, what they're likely to do, and just how far they'll get" (xiv).

The life stories in this volume speak against the dominant master narratives of success, in which triumphant individuals, especially in the sciences, begin their rigorous training in childhood and hail from households with educated parents who carefully cultivate their children's scientific interests and education. The contributors to this volume speak of starts and stalls, of making ends meet as best they could throughout their education. They speak of sacrifices—for instance, studying a subject they were not interested in because at least it was an education, or not knowing where their true interests lay because they were not aware such a field of study existed. The contributors' narratives make visible the messiness of their successful educational trajectories and defy the master narratives of success. Simultaneously, there are many similarities in the contributors' narratives that illuminate alternative paths to educational achievement, which may help direct future generations of scientists down the road toward their own successes.

The Role of Parents, Extended Family, and Community

> My parents understood the value of education, because they had been denied access to education.
>
> —María Elena Zavala

As noted in the quote, many of the contributors to this book had parents who did not have a high school diploma. This lack of education did not result in neglect of their children's education; rather, their way of engaging was to provide moral and practical guidance in solving everyday problems. As Elizabeth Rodríguez-Johnson recalls, her mother alerted her that, unlike the character Sabrina in the movie of the same name, she would not be rescued by a wealthy man; instead, she would have to create her own success. As small as this detail appears on the surface, it is a powerful counternarrative to the master narrative usually given to women: they are all Cinderellas awaiting their handsome Prince Charming to rescue them from poverty, oppression, and ignorance. In this narrative, a woman's role is to be virtuous, pleasant, and patient enough to wait for the charming prince's arrival. Instead, Elizabeth learned, as she states in her history, that the "hero lies in me."

Another contributor, Lydia Villa-Komaroff, looked to the different women in her family and found that each taught her a life lesson. From her maternal grandmother and her great-aunt, both of whom taught in one-room schools in New Mexico, she learned "how satisfying independence could be." From another woman in her family, one who did not have biological children, she learned that "women need not be mothers to be happy and fulfilled." The contributors, from early in their lives, had the characteristics of expert scientists, scanning their environment, picking the best examples of what they desired to be, and deducing the principle that would allow them to live a fulfilling life as a person and as a professional. There are many examples in the contributors' life stories of parents' and relatives' wisdom in countering the master narratives of success and providing the contributors with nontraditional scaffolding for academic achievement.

All of the contributors assert that their parents were extremely supportive of their educational efforts and placed a high value on education. This is surprising and noteworthy, because most master narratives about educational achievement among people of Color claim that these communities do not value education and that their children have to fight tooth and nail to overcome parental objections to their commitment to achieve educationally. The parents' support of their children's educational objectives took various forms. Some were as simple as parents allowing their children to explore their intellectual interests; others were as explicit as providing resources for their children's educational pursuits. Most support, however, consisted of nontraditional "intellectual scaffolding," such as permitting long hours in the library instead of requiring household chores, making intellectual connections among everyday activities such as farming, and avoiding comparisons to brothers and sisters and their educational accomplishments.

Most of the contributors' parents had little or no experience with higher education, and yet they helped their children break the cycle of noneducation by facilitating their academic achievement. But it was not only parents who helped catapult the contributors of this volume to success. These writers existed in larger communities that included aunts, uncles, cousins, grandparents, and siblings. At one time or another, some members of these larger communities also supported the contributors by giving them concrete material resources (like money), providing child care, helping them with college applications, providing temporary housing when they were away from home, affirming their educational choices through attendance at graduations, mentioning their successes to other family members, or telling them how proud they were of their accomplishments.

From these counternarratives of success, a complex picture emerges of what it takes for any individual to overcome huge personal and societal obstacles to be successful academically. Perhaps the largest lesson learned from these essays is that it does indeed take a village to successfully raise a child. It is a lesson not lost on the contributors as they, too, continue the cycle of helping not only their children but also their students, relatives, and colleagues climb the educational ladder.

The Importance of Teachers and Mentors

> One of my junior high teachers, Laura Beheler, remained a friend as we both moved on to high school. . . . When I was ready to go to college, she called me and took me to meet a friend of hers.
>
> —Lydia Villa-Komaroff

All of the contributors to this volume can remember one teacher, if not many, who provided encouragement, guidance, affirmation, and, at times, financial support. The contributors can recall some of these teachers by name, and many have had lifelong relationships with them.

The educational system as a whole may not have always encouraged the contributors to succeed, and, at times, some teachers even discouraged their aspirations, but all can point to at least one teacher who made a difference in their lives. In many instances, the teachers who cared had no idea how important they were in the contributors' lives. Many times these teachers provided seemingly small acts of kindness, such as suggesting to the student that she consider college because of her outstanding performance. Sometimes they helped bridge the knowledge gap about higher education or facilitated the transition from high school to college, college to graduate school, or even graduate school to postgraduate work. If that supportive individual had not taken the time, many of the contributors believe, their lives would have turned out very differently. One of the most important lessons to emerge from this set of writings is how the teachers' small acts of kindness and caring made an enormous difference in the students' educational trajectories.

The Importance of Reading

> I do remember how happy I was to take out books again. Through reading, I could cook anything, learn anything, go anywhere, and be anyone. I still get great pleasure from reading, and from letting the authors take me to faraway places.
> —María Elena Zavala

Access to books and reading was also a crucial aspect of the contributors' academic successes. Many of the contributors mention with great fondness the first books that made an impression on them, such as the Nancy Drew mystery series. Books and reading allowed contributors to imagine worlds beyond the confines of their homes and communities. Here, too, parents were crucial in encouraging and affirming their children's interests in reading. Parents took them to libraries, did not limit the number of books they checked out, and provided space within the home to read.

As seen in the chapters that follow, the contributors read widely, beyond their interests in the sciences, exploring novels, poetry, travel memoirs, and art. In addition to being scientists, the contributors are well read, cultured, and worldly individuals who bring a humanistic bent to their teaching and their lives because they read so much and so broadly from an early age.

Negotiation of Stigma: Racism, Sexism, Classism

We don't have to have our spirits broken to succeed.
—Cleopatria Martínez

The women writers of this book started school with a positive view of themselves and of their communities. Gradually they discovered that who they were—that is, their history, culture, and language—was rarely addressed in their schooling. Many had to learn about their backgrounds on their own in order to restore a positive self-image and refute the stigma they felt for being poor, women, and Mexican. Elizabeth Rodríguez-Johnson poignantly reveals that her low self-esteem was finally lifted when she learned about the contributions Mexicans had made to this country's history. She said that her discovery of Mexican American history gave her "a sense of place and of being who I am."

Several of the contributors to this volume attended institutions of higher education when it was still regarded a minor miracle to find women, even more so Mexican women, at universities. Not surprisingly, several were told directly that higher education was not appropriate for women because, after all, they would soon abandon their careers and get married. This was the case for Elma González when she visited the University of Texas, Austin, while considering an offer to attend their doctoral program in zoology.

The contributors to this volume developed various adaptations to manage the prejudice and discrimination they experienced. Several of them decided early in their lives to ignore obstacles and proceed on their paths to educational achievement. Others decided to confront individuals who they felt were unfair and prejudiced. Still others decided that being the first Chicana botanist, chemist, zoologist, or other scientist was to create a new role. As María Elena Zavala cleverly put it, "On some level, I can never look 'right' as the first Chicano or Chicana to earn a PhD in botany at the University of California, Berkeley, or the first Chicana PhD botanist in the country. How can I determine how I should look?… My botanist models were always whites and mostly males." Professor Zavala decided, as did several other contributors, to create new paths and new styles for being a scientist to overcome prejudice and discrimination.

No matter what adaptation the contributors devised to overcome obstacles as women, Chicanas, first in their families to attend college, and so on, there was obviously a price to pay. Nonetheless, none of the women in this book expresses regret at having taken the "road less traveled"; instead, they marvel at their good fortune to have followed their passions and become scientists, mathematicians, or engineers.

Structure of the Book

This volume is divided into three parts: *Abriendo Caminos* (Opening Roads), *Al Norte* (To the North), and *Pasos con Veredas* (Established Tracks). The first two parts contain three contributed chapters each, and the third part contains four. The parts are not intended to be mutually exclusive, but to provide a means for the reader to connect with the writings in an overarching way.

Abriendo Caminos

The overarching theme of the opening section, *Abriendo Caminos,* is the daunting task faced by the three contributors—the opening of new roads as their parents made enormous sacrifices so they could succeed educationally. All three are the first in their families to finish high school, to attend college, to obtain advanced degrees, and ultimately to become academics. *Abriendo Caminos* is about opening roads previously closed to them and their families.

Al Norte

Of the ten contributors to the volume, almost all in one way or another have experienced migrating *al Norte* to work in the farm fields or in academia. The phrase *al Norte* is used in both Latin and Central America and Mexico, as well as in the United States, to designate the departure of individuals and families from their homelands to pursue employment, opportunities, and, in the case of our contributors, education in *el Norte*. Other racial groups, such as African Americans, have pursued similar opportunities as they left their homes in the South and went "north."

El Norte has become a living metaphor for crossing many types of borders—geographic, educational, social, and economic. Several of the contributors went *al Norte* from their homes in the Southwest to pursue higher education. Ironically, while several of the contributors had gone north as children and young adults *a la pizca* (to harvest fruits and vegetables), later they traveled north to harvest ideas and opportunities. Unlike the *pizcas* of their childhoods, when they migrated with their parents and community members, this time they left family and support system behind as they headed north. There were many anxieties in leaving the security of their families and comforts of their communities. There was also loneliness and the fear of becoming disconnected from everyone and everything familiar to them. Ultimately, all of the contributors who went north succeeded academically; most returned to the Southwest to live close to their families, and all felt enriched by the experience.

Pasos con Veredas

There were four contributors whose families had more experience with higher education than the other families. In these cases, they had parents and siblings who had, at the very least, finished high school and had possibly attended college. For these contributors, usually because they were the youngest in their families or had an older sibling, the road to higher education was not as unknown and challenging as it was for the rest. They followed a pathway laid before them by others in their families. Through family members, these contributors experienced mentorship—*abriendo veredas* (laying down tracks)—so that they did not have to start afresh. As educated family members build on each successive generation, a cycle of educational achievement is created and, moreover, social change is attained.

These contributors' educational experiences were less stressful than those of the other contributors. However, despite their easier routes to education and career, they have always felt a strong commitment to helping others succeed educationally. They understand that their paths were somewhat anomalous when compared with those of other Chicanas and Chicanos, and they are as committed as the other contributors to facilitating students' access to higher education.

Summary

When we gathered in San Antonio, Texas, for the second meeting for this project, the contributors to this book took turns discussing and reading what they planned to write for this volume. As a social psychologist who has studied the educational trajectories of Chicanos for almost two decades, I found myself interrupting often to stress how extraordinary their successes were in light of previously published statistics on the education of Chicanos. According to the data, these women were not supposed to succeed; even those with some advantages far exceeded what social scientists would have predicted for them and their families. Their responses were telltale: they looked at me with a twinkle in their eye, somewhat sorry for my excitement. Repeatedly, they said, "I was just living my life," "I was following my passion," "I was lucky," "I had someone who took an interest in me and mentored me to achieve the next step," "My parents always expected me to succeed in school." Their sense of the ordinariness of their lives is not unusual. Arthur Golden, the author of the very successful fictionalized biography *Memoirs of a Geisha* (1997), notes:

> A memoir provides a record not so much of the memoirist as of the memoirist's world.... Autobiography, if there is really such a thing, is like asking a rabbit to tell us what he [sic] looks like hopping the grasses of the field. How would he [sic] know? If we want to hear about the field, on the other hand, no one is in a better circumstance to tell us—so long as we keep in mind that we are missing all those things the rabbit was in no position to observe. (1–2)

The contributors to this volume have led extraordinary lives, achieved extraordinary achievements, and are extraordinary human beings. At the same time, they see their lives as ordinary, fulfilling, and achievable by anybody who puts her mind and heart to it. The message that rings loud and clear is "You, too, can do it, because I did and I'm no different from you." There couldn't be a more hopeful message for those searching for their own passions and *veredas* into the future.

Works Cited

Delgado, Richard. 1995. "Legal Storytelling: Storytelling for Oppositionists and Others: A Plea for Narrative." In *Critical Race Theory: The Cutting Edge*, ed. Richard Delgado, 54–74. Philadelphia: Temple University Press.

Golden, Arthur. 1997. *Memoirs of a Geisha*. New York: Vintage Books.

Romero, Mary, and Abigail Stewart, eds. 1999. *Women's Untold Stories: Breaking Silence, Talking Back, Voicing Complexity*. New York: Routledge.

Part I
Abriendo Caminos

CHAPTER 1

What I Did on My Summer Vacation

Elma González
*Professor Emerita of
Ecology and
Evolutionary Biology*

I stopped having summer vacations after my thirteenth birthday, in 1955. That was the year my father met Mr. Manuel Flores of Zapata, Texas. Mr. Flores was a *troquero,* which, literally translated from Spanglish, means truck driver, but in fact the title meant a lot more to us. Mr. Flores was a migrant labor boss whose job was to recruit and deliver farmworkers for a commission to farmers and the enterprises that bought their crops in the Midwest. Since before World War II, recruiters had operated all over south Texas and contracted thousands of farmworker families for work in *el Norte.*

Mr. Flores had six nearly grown or adult children. He was also related by blood, marriage, or friendship to a number of other workers who made up the core of his labor gang. I can remember only his younger children, Salvador (always Shava) and Irma, who were close to my age. One of his older sons had recently returned from the Korean War. For some years, Mr. Flores had loaded his family and their migrant household essentials onto his three-ton flatbed truck with blue wooden five-foot railings, and led a convoy of cars and trucks to *el Norte* for *las pizcas* (the crop harvests).

After my father's meeting with Mr. Flores, my family went to nearby Zapata from our home in Hebbronville, Texas, to learn more about the migrant experience. At that first meeting, the Flores family came across as prosperous. They greeted us warmly at their new ranch-style home with its many bedrooms. I was impressed by the apparent wealth these people enjoyed. They showed slides of the people they

had worked for during their previous summers. I noticed their new movie camera and projection screen, and I was amazed because I had never seen home movies before. I remember the souvenirs their son had sent from Korea: colorful cushions with embroidered dragons, a sword, and other knick-knacks, all wonderfully exotic to me. My parents were more impressed with the Flores family's integrity, sound values, and goodwill. After much discussion, my parents "signed us up," and we

Elma González, age 2, with her aunt, Guadalupe Lopez, and cousin Sylvia Lopez, in Laredo, Texas, 1944.

began to make plans for the season ahead, which would take us first to Colorado and later to Wisconsin.

In their large, comfortable kitchen, Mrs. Flores and her daughters entertained my mother and other visiting women, effortlessly preparing lunch for a large group of people. Mom wanted to know the details of the traveling kit we would need to take for the four or more months on the road. Mrs. Flores demonstrated how to pack your traveling coffee-pot (old and banged up), enameled plates and cups (one for each family member), cutlery, skillet, a couple of pots, and other kitchen essentials into a large tin tub. Along with the washboard, the tub was primarily for washing the family laundry, but it also doubled as a bath-tub. The largest kitchen item was the stove—a three-burner, kerosene unit that produced copious amounts of soot and was difficult to regu-late. The remainder of the traveling kit was made up of our clothing and bedding. Sufficient *colchas* (comforters) and blankets would be needed, because we assumed that beds would be mostly unavailable and that it would be cold by the end of the season. As cruel experience would teach us later, those blankets were never thick enough after a day's hard work, when we bedded down on packed dirt, rough boards, or concrete. Clothing for the season ahead was minimal, two pairs of jeans and shirts for work for each of us, and maybe a Saturday dress for me and my sisters. For the six in our family, our entire kit for the four months probably took up less than sixty cubic feet of space, or about what you could pack in the cargo space of an SUV.

Mrs. Flores and her girls emphasized the harsh effects of the sun on our complexions, so among the most important garments for work in the fields was *el garsolé* (the lady's pioneer bonnet). This hellish head covering was carefully home-constructed of cloth and cardboard. The long tube in front of the face provided maximum protection from the sun. Equally important were the cloth gloves and sturdy long-sleeved shirt that we were to wear at all times in the fields. The bonnet would become the hardest garment to get used to because it blocked airflow and magnified the heat of the day. It also confined your view to a small area in front of your feet. But the bonnet did protect my mother and me (my sisters were still too young for fieldwork) against excessive sunburn, and, in all probability, reduced our risk for melanoma. In later years, large straw hats replaced the bonnets.

Before starting out on the long trek north, the gathering point was the Flores home in Zapata. Usually we were picked up by their truck at our house in Hebbronville on the same day that schoolchildren were released for the summer break. We anticipated the adventure with great excitement. We said good-bye to our friends and bragged about (or hid) our report cards, all the while trying to help load the truck. There were important last-minute details for securing our little house, which was to remain empty for such a long period. Although we never owned pets, my sister was always concerned about a favorite stray cat or two left with one house less to appeal to for handouts. The neighbors came to wave good-bye, worried about us, and urged us to write. If they thought we were crazy for taking such risks, they politely kept those thoughts to themselves, or from our ears at least.

Later that night in Zapata, the Flores clan went through the same preparations. They were more experienced at packing, and their lives seemed more glamorous and complex than ours. More of their family and friends came by to say good-bye. Eventually, the hubbub calmed down for the night. Sleep didn't come so easily for children or adults. The children's excitement was not easily contained: some expressed fear, and some only saw the beginning of an adventure. Parents worried. We began our northward trek at first light the next morning.

With children half asleep and disoriented, each family quickly climbed on board and found a cramped bit of space amid bundles of bedding and the bodies of relatives and strangers. As the truck and the following caravan moved north, we sat and passed the time as well as we could, or slumped down to sleep and endure the journey for the next four or five days.

Most of the men would take turns driving and sleeping. The route was familiar to the Flores drivers, but others, like my dad, were inexperienced drivers and not comfortable reading the highway signs. Many of the other fellows lacked spare drivers in their cars and pickups, and so were constantly fighting exhaustion. There were bathroom breaks every few hours, depending on the availability of roadside rest areas, and typically a halt was called at midnight, either along the road or at some other convenient open area, where the adults quickly unrolled bedding, disentangled children, and attempted to sleep on the roadside grass for a few hours. Our strange troop sometimes caught the attention of the local police, but I can't recall any truly unpleasant episode of harassment. In that world the men were in charge, and we assumed that our fathers and brothers were able to deal with such and other encounters.

However, there was something that neither the men nor anyone else could control, and that was the late spring weather of the American Midwest. It was a daunting experience to travel in rainy and/or cold weather. In south Texas, we thought of the end of May as the beginning of our hot summer weather, but as we moved north through Oklahoma and Colorado, we encountered true spring weather, which was quite nippy by our standards, especially at night and early in the morning. Worse yet was the return trip in late September or early October, when it could be wet and below freezing at night. The truck bed, covered by a tarp, carried the traveling kits of four to six families, with twenty to twenty-five children and adults sitting on bedrolls in the semidarkness. During the hotter days, the sun beat down mercilessly on the dark green tarp, driving the temperature to brutal levels. The heat also compounded the constant discomfort generated by traffic exhaust fumes, the chemicals released by the treated tarp over our heads, and the body odors and uneasy stomachs of the travelers—an unwelcome malodorous cocktail indeed.

Wet weather was its own special hell. When it rained continuously for several days, there was no way to dry the damp bedding, nor was there likely to be a suitable stopping place for a few hours of rest. Later, we would have to contend with the damp and unpleasant odor of mildew. People's tempers became ragged, and bickering might escalate to blows, although full-fledged fistfights were rare. In the four years we traveled with the Flores family, I can recall only a single occasion when two matrons lost it, started pounding each other, and were quickly separated. These moments were especially hard on my parents, because their first instinct was to shelter their children from unpleasantness and rough language.

In those early years, our destination was either eastern Colorado or southern Nebraska along the Platte River. At both locations, the work was in the sugar beet fields and under contract to the Great Western Sugar Company. In early June, the beet plants were mere seedlings and required both thinning and weeding. Those were the days of the infamous "short" hoes, often described as one of the worst implements devised to torture the farmworker. Its reputation is well deserved. *El cortito* is an ordinary hoe with a shortened handle, approximately twelve to fourteen inches long. It is operated with one hand, while the worker continues to chop and move sideways along the row of plants in a stooped position, with his or her head about two and a half feet above the ground.

In 1975, Governor Jerry Brown of California forwarded an administrative ruling that banned the use of the *cortito* from California agriculture. Today, agricultural technologies, in concert with agricultural economics, have nearly rendered such labor-intensive practices obsolete. New tools and technologies sow one seed at a time, so that the crops no longer require thinning. During those days, thinning the seedlings was essential, because the isolated beet plant normally develops a storage root that enlarges to twelve or more inches across as it accumulates sugar. When two or more seedlings remain together, they inhibit one another's expansion. Weeding is now done chemically in a relatively safe and inexpensive manner. Recombinant DNA technology has introduced herbicide resistance to many crops. Thus, it is possible now to use herbicides that will not harm the crop plant but will rid the fields of the weeds we once removed with a hoe. However, the demand for "organic" produce, and suspicion of genetically modified crops in general, have resulted in a resurgence of the short hoe and hand weeding for lettuce, broccoli, strawberries, and other delicate but highly profitable crops. The struggle to protect farmworkers' health continues in California and elsewhere.

The work in the beet fields was paid by the acre. The contract stipulated two passes; the first pass was for thinning and weeding the seedlings, and the second, done about three weeks later, was for weeding the more mature plants with a long hoe. The pay to the farmworker for this monthlong effort was approximately twenty-five dollars per acre. Our family (father, mother, brother, and I) was able to cover a very modest number of acres during our first year, but by the second year, when my brother and I were older and my parents more savvy, we collected pay for about eighteen or twenty acres for the month of June. When you do piecework, you cannot afford to take many breaks to ease your painful back. Too little ground covered reaps too little pay. The alternative was to negotiate for hourly wages that, at fifty to sixty-five cents per hour, resulted in an even more meager paycheck. To make matters worse, some of the fields were too dry and the soil very hard, especially for young wrists and hands, or were overrun by tough grasses and weeds, which slowed the work considerably. Much depended on the farmer's skill in cultivating the crop, and his timing with respect to planting and irrigation. Workers with prior experience could anticipate which fields and which farmers were to be avoided, if possible.

The best way to endure the long, hot, sweaty hours was to match the working pace of a friend or relative, so that you could talk, tell stories, or sing across the rows. There were no restrooms. You were lucky if the field was near a woodsy area. In an emergency, the women would create a makeshift privacy screen using coats and tarps. Sometimes we resorted to refusing water to avoid having to relieve ourselves.

The workday followed the sunup-to-sundown rule, so there were at least ten hours of very hard labor Monday through Friday, and half a day on Saturday for everyone aged twelve and up. My father's *descanso con honra* (honorable rest) was reserved for rainy days. Saturday was bath day, made possible only if you remembered, before starting for work, to leave a *cubeta* or *bañito* with two or three gallons of water out in the sun. At quitting time, this warm water would be taken to a space set aside for bathing privacy, for a quick bath *a mocasos*—that is, with an enameled metal cup, or with a beaker made from a tin soup can and a wire handle. While the women stayed home to wash clothes, the men and teenage daughters ventured out to the nearby town to do the marketing for the week. Some of the men also chose to celebrate the end of the week at the local bars. Fortunately for us, the Flores work gang was a fairly sober bunch, and not likely to attract the unwanted attention of the local authorities. Most of us saw intimidating signs, such as "No dogs or Mexicans allowed," in some of the shops and restaurants in west

Texas. Such visible expression of prejudice kept our contact with the locals to a minimum.

The last leg of our northward migration began around the Fourth of July, after we finished working in Nebraska or Colorado. During the first two or three years of my family's migrant experience, the work troop then headed for the Oconto Valley of eastern Wisconsin. The Flores family had been working cucumber fields for the same farmers in this area for some years, and they had warm relationships with many of the growers. My family was placed with the Spellers, a Scandinavian American family with a field of cucumbers, which we picked daily for the pickling plant. Cucumber vines were not staked, but sprawled along wide rows, requiring the worst kind of stoop labor. You had to lift the heavy, interlaced plants a short distance from the ground to see the small, tender cucumbers. The crop was picked on an every-other-day schedule, rain or shine, because the consistent harvesting of the smallest, or gherkin, sizes paid better than the larger ones. You could not afford to ignore your allotted rows. We wore long latex gloves through the hot summer days to avoid the tiny but very sharp spines of the fresh cucumbers. In addition to the constant stooping to reach the vines at ground level, each of us had to move an iron, five-gallon collection bucket forward along the row. Sometimes, when backs became too painful, pickers advanced along the rows on padded knees. However, because younger children do not have much upper body strength, we had difficulty moving forward while on our knees, even when the bucket was only half full. The buckets were emptied approximately every fifty feet into burlap bags, which were collected at the end of the day for the trip to the pickling plant. Occasional but painful encounters with honeybees from the rented hives located at midfield were an unexpected minor hazard. Honeybees are necessary for pollination of some crops and ensure abundant plant productivity. Fortunately, domestic honeybees don't attack unless they feel threatened.

Despite the very real physical hardship of this labor, it was outdoor work in the fresh, clean air. Unlike cotton, which we also harvested on occasion, the edible crops were less likely to be sprayed with pesticides, herbicides, or defoliants. In those days, the work was not as mechanized as it is today, so we were not often exposed to the dangers of having to work around heavy machinery. Needless to say, none of us was covered by medical insurance.

The greatest hardship we suffered during those years was the exceedingly primitive, unsanitary, overcrowded, and sometimes disgusting living conditions we endured. Of course, every year and every situation was different. For the most part, the grower or farmer was responsible for housing his migrant labor. When we were lucky, we were moved into old farmhouses that had been residences in the (one hoped) not too distant past. The good places had roofs that did not leak, indoor water (either a pump or a spigot), and more or less hygienic, well-maintained outhouses. Sometimes there were fruit trees; I remember a wonderful large apple tree next to the farmhouse where we stayed somewhere in Michigan. Delectable Golden Delicious apples were an unexpected treat. Occasionally, when the farmers and migrants enjoyed an exceptionally warm relationship, the farmer prepared for the season by planting a vegetable garden for his migrant family.

Sometimes farmers offered their workers primitive but clean and dry single shelters detached from other families. I remember one such place in Nebraska, in the middle of a wheat field. The vast field of unripe wheat was whipped about into furious waves by the wind during violent thunderstorms. I appreciated the lush, abstract beauty of such scenes. Those moments were the perfect backdrop for my fantasy life, dreams of a life that would not include the hard work of the migrant field hand. Mostly, I thought of myself as leading an interesting life away from the farms and small towns of my experience. Another habitation I remember was a farmhouse very close to the shallows of the Platte River, where, on Sundays, under the majestic cottonwoods, we floated on old inflated inner tubes, spinning daydreams.

My most memorable experience occurred in the midst of the Nebraska prairie during the several days we stayed in an abandoned, single-room schoolhouse. Several families were given temporary shelter there, and my family ended up in a corner where old discarded schoolbooks were piled up. What joy! I read and read, but as much as I pleaded, my parents would not let me take any of the books when we left. Those were old readers, textbooks from the turn of the twentieth century, with stories, poems, and etchings of famous paintings. Many years later, at the Metropolitan Museum of Art in New York, I unexpectedly turned the corner into one of the galleries to confront a huge painting, *The Horse Fair*, by Rosa Bonheur. I experienced "gooseflesh" as I remembered seeing the small etching of this painting in one of those readers in the Nebraska schoolhouse fifteen years before.

Some of the accommodations were truly awful—so much so that fifty years later they are still featured in my worst dreams. Some camps housed people from different migrant groups. Some were disorderly and disruptive: alcohol and marijuana were not unknown. You could easily hear slapping and cursing through thin walls. In one case, we spent the summer on the second floor of a rickety building that housed a pigsty on the first floor. The smell and the flies were nightmarish. As usual, my parents tried their best to shield us from the worst living conditions.

The harvests of *el Norte* were pretty much complete by early September. Most of the families accompanying the Flores family had schoolchildren, and they wanted to return home. However, the troop sometimes extended the season by looking for "opportunities." One such call came for workers to harvest a crop of overripe tomatoes that was threatened by early frost in Illinois. The desperate farmers were paying a premium wage. I remember this experience most vividly, because one morning, as we sat on our buckets at the edge of the field, waiting for enough light to see the smelly tomatoes, I distinctly remember promising myself that I would become educated so that I would never, ever have to get up at that hour of the morning to do such awful work.

Finally, with jubilation and a few dollars saved, we would head back to south Texas. During the first four years of the nine years we followed the migrant routes, we returned home five to six weeks after the start of the school year. Although my siblings and I were never held back a grade because of our absences at the beginning of the school year, my parents were not happy about our having to miss school. By the beginning of my sophomore year in high school, in 1958, my father had bought an old car to follow the Flores convoy. The car gave us the option of starting home earlier, in time for the beginning of the school year, even when the gang wanted to extend the season.

The summer of 1961 was the last one we spent outside Texas. I can recall someone handing me the letter of admission to college while I was on a ladder picking cherries in one of the orchards of the Upper Traverse Peninsula in Michigan. By the end of 1961, my parents had decided to stop following the Flores migrant troop, and concentrate on work in the cotton fields in northwest Texas. Working the cotton fields entailed weeding the young plants, not picking the ripe bolls, which was much easier work. More important, weeding was completed by mid-August. This change in our migration pattern made an important difference to our schooling. The change became possible because my younger sisters were now hourly wage earners (at sixty-five cents an hour, who could not afford to hire a child?). Now the six of us, working long hours, five and a half days a week, earned enough money to buy the clothes, shoes, and supplies to keep us in school for the year. This goal was what the whole experience had been about—to keep us in school for as long as possible.

During the nine summers we traveled north, we logged thousands of miles and saw a large section of the country. We worked in or passed through Oklahoma, Colorado, Kansas, Iowa, Wisconsin, Michigan, Illinois, South Dakota, and many parts of Texas. We harvested or tended a large variety of crops, including sugar beets, cucumbers, green beans, tomatoes, cotton, cherries, and sorghum. We learned a lot about the good, the bad, and the ugly among our *compañeros*. We benefited from the friendship extended by workers and bosses alike. We also saw or were aware of cheats, wife-beaters, sexual predators, *marigüanos*, and other riffraff.

Why did my parents put us through this? They did it because there were no other viable choices. We are lucky that our parents believed so fervently in education. I have never heard my siblings bemoan these experiences or blame our parents because we missed out on the typical fun of a child's summer vacation. Although we griped and protested at the time, we knew that to stay in school we had to pull together as a family in the only way available to us.

Despite all the hardships, I learned many valuable lessons during those summers. I learned that hard work under safe and sanitary conditions can be satisfying, and that such work teaches endurance and discipline. Thus, hard work has never frightened me. Perhaps more important, I learned that the economic rewards of physical labor are disproportionate to the hardships and dangers suffered by the worker. At the very least, these experiences motivated us to stay in school and eventually seek better ways to make a living.

Mentors

I've been fortunate to have many mentors who have influenced my life. Because I was able to extract a good deal of information about life and living from the books I read, I consider the reading of certain books as mentoring experiences. In particular, biographies, autobiographies (yes, even *True Confessions*), and literary novels taught me a great deal about life, about decisions people make and how they make them, and about the world outside my hometown. The stories of Anton Chekhov made me wonder how his angst-ridden aristocrats could drown in teacups. I couldn't help contrasting the idle, educated Russian landowners to people like us. They were miserable, and we had the capacity to enjoy life. My reading taught me that much of what happens to us is perceived and filtered through our values, expectations, and sense of self-worth. My parents' values, my sense of security within the family, my reading, and my own personality contributed to my ability to filter out the negative and dwell on the positive and hopeful. I don't think I was aware of the cliché that urges you to make lemonade if all you have are lemons. However, I had thought through my own explanation of why I could see the world differently.

By the age of seventeen, I had conceived of my theory of personality. I wanted to account for the differences that determined why one person could transcend his or her environment and another, despite all the advantages that family and society could offer, could be vulnerable. I wrote in my diary that an analogy useful for figuring out this conundrum was that of the sculptor and his medium. The sculptor could be clumsy and lacking talent, or be very gifted; his or her choice of medium could range from the delicate alabaster and terra-cotta to the hard and durable marble. I reasoned that a genius could create art from any medium, but that the clumsy sculptor (with limited talent) might succeed with marble but not with more delicate materials.

According to my theory, our personalities are analogous to the sculptor's medium and the sculptor is analogous to our environment. I had basically arrived at the elements of the "nature vs. nurture" debates on my own. Of course, I decided that I was marble and that I would become "a work of art," regardless of how clumsy my "sculptor" might be. While this analogy may sound self-aggrandizing, it really was useful to me as I began to accept my "different-ness."

At about the time that I was struggling to resolve the conflict between my ambition to pursue an education and the expectations of my family, I had a fortuitous conversation with my high school principal. He asked me whether I would be going to college, and I enumerated the many barriers: no money, my family's expectation for my help, no one in my family had been to college, and so on. He said I reminded him of his mother, who had never had the chance to go to college and had become "a very bitter old woman." For some reason, at that moment I could "see" the future, and knew that I too could become a very bitter old woman. After that, there was no question in my mind about college. I did everything in my power to make it a reality. I even staged a tearful encounter to get my father to cosign my student loan documents.

After four years at the Texas Woman's University, where I double-majored in biology and chemistry, and completed a credential for teaching biology and chemistry in high school, I was unprepared and unwilling to take a teaching offer in a small, dusty town in southwest Texas. Fortunately, I had spent the previous summer as a student intern at the Baylor University College of Medicine, doing research in the Department of Pharmacology. I had taken this job as a way of making a final break with the migrant labor experience. It was an exhilarating summer, despite the hardship of having no money for food until I was finally paid at the end of the month. This experience was my first exposure to research, and I quickly understood that this was something I really wanted to do with my life. It also helped that the people I worked for wanted me to apply to their graduate school right then (without going back to finish my senior year). I understood this to mean that they believed I really had the talent and preparation for a career in research—it was no longer just my private pipe dream.

Thus, as I was about to receive my degree and still did not have a job, a very casual look at the positions listed in the *Dallas Morning News* led me to a job as a research technician at the University of Texas Southwestern Medical School. I worked in that capacity for three years and made monthly monetary contributions to my family. The job experience was valuable but frustrating. Although I learned research techniques and absorbed the culture of the research environment, by the end of those three years I was impatient with my limited education, which did not allow me to fully understand the experiments. It also seemed that when the experiments succeeded, it was my boss's genius that made them work, and when they did not, it was my fault.

I applied to several graduate schools, including the University of Texas, Austin, where, through the efforts of another female technician at the medical school, I was granted an interview with one of the faculty in the zoology department. I drove to Austin in a dense fog, through terrible traffic, and arrived with a splitting headache. I spoke with several faculty members, but none of the interviews went well. I told a biochemistry professor that I wanted to study biochemistry, but "not the kind of biochemistry where you spend your whole life on one enzyme!" Only too late did I realize that he had studied a single enzyme for twenty years—not an uncommon practice at that time. Another faculty member asked me what I "wanted." When I responded "a PhD," he urged me to consider "who you are" and that for a woman who was probably going to get married, a doctorate was not a practical ambition. Even in 1967, I was amazed that he would make such blatantly sexist comments. Unfortunately, such sexist and racist attitudes had intimidated many Chicanas from making further attempts to continue their education. Despite this experience, the University of Texas did offer me admission, but it placed me on an alternate list for financial aid.

I mostly applied to out-of-state graduate schools because, as I told everyone, I wanted to see "how the other half lives." I was accepted by Rutgers University's program in cellular biology and awarded a teaching assistantship. I drove my '65 Mustang all the way to New Jersey and looked for modest lodging. I found a room in the home of a woman whose children were grown and out of the house. I came to know the Pollack family very well, and we have remained friends over the years. For me they embodied "the other half": educated Jewish intellectuals who enjoyed loud and heated political discussions. Since I was raised with the saying "Sticks and stones may break my bones but words will never hurt me" ringing in my ear, I was at first puzzled by the attention the Pollacks paid to the Nixon speeches published in the *New York Times.* Gradually I began to appreciate that "words" that become law or policy are far more important to society or a community than I had realized.

My professor at Rutgers, Charlotte Avers, was a great influence on me—first, because she was a woman (and thus a female role model), and second, because she was tough. She gave meaning to the phrase "doesn't tolerate fools gladly." Although Charlotte intimidated many, she was always fair, and her style of teaching motivated me. Basically, she encouraged her graduate students to solve problems on their own. While difficult at first, I learned the fundamentals and how to ask the right research questions. Just as I was finishing my graduate work, Charlotte asked me about my plans. When I answered that I would be going back to Texas to teach at a community college, she exclaimed, "What! You have to postdoc. Everyone is doing it!" Thus, I wrote a proposal and applied for a National Institutes of Health (NIH) postdoctoral fellowship.

In 1969, my first year in graduate school, the New York Academy of Sciences in Manhattan had hosted a symposium titled "Microbodies, Peroxisomes, and Glyoxysomes." Charlotte took her graduate students to that meeting, where we were exposed to cutting-edge work in this subfield of cell biology. Among the scientists presenting papers were Harry Beevers, then at Purdue University, and Christian de Duve of the Rockefeller University. Later, when Charlotte insisted that I apply for a postdoc position, I read up on my favorite topics and developed a short proposal that I submitted as part of my application for the NIH postdoctoral fellowship. I wrote letters of introduction and inquiry to three or four heads of laboratories whose work interested me, among them Professors Beevers and de Duve.

Christian de Duve granted me an interview in Manhattan. That was a huge deal for me. Professor de Duve had one lab at the Rockefeller and another at the Catholic University in Louvain. He had big lab groups at both institutes and split his residency between Belgium and New York. During my interview, he and his lab colleagues took me to lunch at the sumptuous University Club. I barely touched my lunch because they asked me so many questions about my work. I was in seventh heaven. I would have loved to do my postdoctoral research in Europe, but de Duve had no openings in his European lab; he had hundreds of applications even for his New York lab. The following year, de Duve and two other scientists received the Nobel Prize in Physiology.

I had also written to Professor Harry Beevers, who was by then at the University of California, Santa Cruz (UCSC). His group worked on an organelle that I thought might serve as a good research model for investigating some of the questions that interested me. My studies on yeast peroxisomes had led me to question how newly synthesized enzymes might be directed to their specific sites in the cell. Although Beevers accepted me for a postdoc in his lab, his letter was very brief, and I wanted his opinion of the work I had proposed in the NIH fellowship application. Quite opportunely, the Rutgers undergraduates chartered a flight to San Francisco for spring break in 1972, so I was able to fly to California to meet Professor Beevers. Harry Beevers had been elected to the National Academy of Sciences in 1969, and his lab hosted an international cohort of postdocs. During my spring break visit, Professor Beevers and Jean, his wife, insisted that I stay with them at their home in Pasatiempo Estates while we talked about my project and I visited with the other members of the lab. By the end of my trip, I was beginning to truly believe in my dream—this daughter of migrant laborers could think of herself as a scientist.

In July 1972, after I defended my dissertation at Rutgers, I returned to Texas and waited to hear from the NIH about my application. Finally, after getting positive news, I drove myself to Santa Cruz in my '65 Mustang, arriving there in December during one of the coldest winters they'd had in years. Through much of January and February, I was cold and hungry because my fellowship stipend was delayed while Rutgers confirmed my degree. Dr. Beevers soon realized my financial straits and lent me money to pay rent, while Professor Jean Langenheim, one of the few women on the science faculty, lent me some sweaters and a blanket. I was lonely, and soon realized I knew next to nothing about plant physiology. Harry Beevers had five other postdocs and a graduate student working with him, and he and Jean were wonderful to us. I gradually felt befriended and valued, and Harry made it clear that my expertise in cell biology was needed in his lab. Although they had very different teaching styles, both Harry and Charlotte Avers believed in giving their students opportunities to contribute creatively and at their own pace.

I began my postdoc experience under a mild depression (analogous to postpartum depression, but in this case "postdoctorate depression"), but the supportive environment and the friendships I found at UCSC were restorative. After a few sessions with a local psychologist, I managed to pull myself out of the dumps and restore my balance. During my first year in Santa Cruz, I was fortunate to come under the protective wing of Professor Gene Cota-Robles, a microbiologist who had recently arrived on campus and had assumed duties on the chancellor's staff. He introduced me to Katia Panas, a Greek Chicana American who was a psychologist in the UCSC counseling services. Katia was a supportive and nurturing person, and her friendship was valuable to

Elma González as a postdoctoral fellow in the Beevers lab at the University of California, Santa Cruz, 1973.

me at a time when I had to make a decision to "go for it"—that is, seek a job at a major university.

All through this period, my parents were mostly at a loss in understanding my career decisions. They never fully grasped the concept of postdoctoral work, nor the reasons the work was so demanding of my time. My father wanted to know why I did not take a vacation. I was finally able to explain by comparing my work as an academic scientist to owning your own business—you could not leave it unattended. My mother simply told people I was a medical technologist, because I had initially gone to college to study medical technology. I had described the field as leading to an occupation with opportunities and good pay. She happily continued to believe this until well after I received my PhD.

Academic Science

Academic positions at research universities are always scarce. The six other postdocs in my lab (all men) were looking for jobs and daily bemoaning their scarcity. The day that I was called for an interview at the University of California, Los Angeles, I jumped at it (although at that point I barely had a year's worth of postdoc experience). When UCLA offered me the position of assistant professor, I had a whole chorus back in Santa Cruz telling me I had to take the job. In retrospect, I could have used more seasoning before tackling the rigors of teaching and research at a major university. I had a total of eighteen years of formal education (ten, four, and four) and a barely adequate twenty-two months as a postdoc. But I was thirty-two years old and anxious to start a *real* job.

Now, in a new red '73 Datsun, I drove down U.S. 101 to Los Angeles, all my worldly possessions in the trunk and in a hamper atop the roof of my car. I moved into a furnished apartment close to campus and started the Byzantine process of making my way in academia. I had not fully appreciated that my appointment was intended to fulfill an affirmative action commitment from the chancellor's office. The department of biology, and particularly the staff, was essentially unaware of my appointment. The immediate problem was finding an office. Finally, someone identified an unoccupied office in the vivarium wing of the Life Sciences building. I didn't mind sharing my corridor with the mice and rabbits so much, because some of the offices in that wing were occupied by acting assistant professors and lecturers close to my age. The tough part was getting a lab assigned to me so that I would have a place for the equipment I could buy with my meager setup funds (even in 1974, fourteen thousand dollars didn't buy much). However, I made the most of those funds by working with the equipment sales-men and buying discounted "demonstration" equipment. I discovered that by asking the salesmen to bid on instrument packages, they could bypass the agreed-upon price contracts with the university and offer much lower prices.

During those first early years, I was befriended by Professor Sam Wildman, an eminent plant biologist famous for his studies on ribu-lose bisphosphate carboxylase/oxygenase (RUBISCO). He understood what it meant to me to not have my own lab space, and he offered me space in his lab and the use of his equipment. Sam continued to be a supportive friend and mentor until the end of his life in 2004, at the age of ninety-two. I was also fortunate to become friends with Larry Simpson and his wife, Agda. They were both about my age, but Larry was much more advanced along his academic path. Larry also lent me equipment for my work, and helped me navigate the depart-ment and university. Larry and I also co-taught a cell biology course for about ten years.

The early 1970s was a period of rapid expansion at the university, and the doors opened for women and people of more diverse ethnic backgrounds. In the sciences, I was one of several female tenure candidates hired at UCLA around the same time and moving up for tenure at about the same pace. Unfortunately, I remained the only Mexican American female scientist in the entire University of California system until the appointment of Dr. Martha Zúñiga at the University of California, Santa Cruz, in 1990. The first seven years in an academic career are truly intense. There are many struggles: start your research, obtain grant funding, face tough and insensitive manuscript and grant proposal reviews, and learn to teach university courses. The hours in the lab are long, and giving in to despair when experiments fail and papers are rejected is common. It is easy to question one's own abilities and intelligence. However, lest it seem that academic life has no redeeming qualities, it is worth noting that there is no feeling quite like the immense elation experienced when a grant is funded, when a published manuscript leads to invitations to speak at national and international symposia, when students return and say you have inspired them, or when someone visits from afar because you are the "world's expert" in your field. When I received tenure, I celebrated by buying a house and a white MGB Roadster.

I was recently reminded that just because something is hard or challenging doesn't mean it's impossible. As a young girl, I enjoyed challenges, and I particularly enjoyed science exactly because it *was* challenging, and also because it nearly always provided the means to satisfy my questions. The challenge and its degree of difficulty depend on the quality of one's preparation to engage the effort. In other words, science is not *easy*, and you can't be a scientist without rigorous intellectual and psychological preparation. Nevertheless, the academic life is challenging and fulfilling in equal measure. After thirty-five years in academia, as I sit and contemplate the past and the choices I made, I have no regrets: I still would choose the same path and the same career.

CHAPTER 2

Haciendo Caras

The Making of a
Scientist

María Elena Zavala
Professor of Biology

When I was very young, my mother was ill. My older brother and sisters were in school, and I had to learn to entertain myself safely. My mother could not always do the things that other mothers did for their young children, such as pick me up from school, or even pick me up when I was hurt. During her worst periods, the most she could do for me was talk with me, and comb and braid my hair. She would tell me stories about her life, her mother, and my great-grandmother. When she became extremely ill and went into the hospital, I worried because I knew that when her mother had died, her grandmother had taken care of her, but both of my grandmothers were dead. I also knew that my mother's father died soon after her mother did, so I was not sure whether that always happened. Whenever my mother had been ill, my older sisters had been responsible for me, and it was no fun at all. I was worried that if my mother died, my

27

older sisters would "take care of me," a phrase that, in our house, conveyed a threat. My sisters also told me that if I misbehaved, my mother could die. I did everything I could to ensure that my mother stayed alive! I was quiet and obedient, worked hard, studied diligently, and prayed. And I made up great adventures in my mind and in my yard to entertain myself.

Our yard was full of different and useful plants and animals. Over the course of my childhood, goats, dogs, chickens, ducks, geese, rabbits, parakeets, and, for a time, even a pet turkey were all part of our menagerie. I asked questions about the plants and animals in our yard. For example, I wanted to know why the peach tree did not have peaches all year long, and why some eggs became fluffy little chicks and others breakfast. I wanted to know why *yerba buena* was both a cooking herb and, in combination with other herbs, a medicine. I was full of questions.

Early Observations

My parents and grandparents did not always have the answers, but they told me to observe the plants and animals, and that maybe they themselves would reveal the answers. I learned to watch the plants and animals go through their life cycles. Once I dissected a whole rosebush full of flowers. That was the only time I suffered a consequence from one of my "experiments." My dad was walking past me and asked what I was doing. I told him I was looking at how the flowers were put together. He asked me if I now knew how they were assembled, and I told him yes. He told me that I should stop taking the flowers apart then, and walked away. I then proceeded to dissect the last two open flowers, my dad returning just as the last petal fell to the ground. He looked at me, furious. He made me clean up every single petal and stamen. As he watched me, he gave me a lecture about obedience, respect for elders and parents, and abusing his goodwill. I knew that when I was finished cleaning up, I was going to be spanked, not for learning from the flowers but for being disobedient. As I expected, my dad spanked me. It was the second and last time that he ever spanked me.

The one meal we ate together as a family was dinner, and we all had to be home for it. After dinner, we were expected to share something about our day. One time, I described the mating behavior of roosters and hens without understanding the intention of their actions. I explained that the rooster was being mean to the hen, and I had tried to chase him off. However, he was persistent, and after a while he chased me away. My parents told me that we could expect eggs soon from the hen, and maybe even chicks. The first skills of a scientist were being nurtured in me by my parents and family; learning how to be a careful observer prepared me for my life's work.

It was no wonder that I conducted my first experiment when I was five or six, in the back of my dad's retired farm laborers' transport truck. I wanted to see whether plants would grow better in the shade or sun. I still remember my first results. The seeds germinated, but I forgot to water them, so they all died. My mother gave me more bean and lentil seeds to try again. She also prepared a jar lined with wet paper towels, and we placed some seeds in it, so I could watch the seeds grow without digging them up and replanting them. I was surprised to see that the shade plants were taller than the sun plants, and also noticed that the tall ones fell over quickly.

My parents encouraged my experiments in every way they could. When I was around eight years old, I started a small fire in the kitchen, trying to make candles out of paraffin and old crayons. Actually, I had first tried to color the wax with food coloring, but that did not work. I then let the wax cool and harden before wiping the food coloring

María Elena Zavala with her mother and father (and rosebush), circa 1956.

off and starting again. The fire started when I became impatient with the rate at which the paraffin was remelting; I decided to speed the process by holding the can with the melting paraffin directly on the stove, rather than leaving it in the water bath as my mother had instructed. A little wax dripped out and caught on fire. More wax then spilled on the stove when I dropped the can, igniting more paraffin. My mother quickly smothered the fire. I had to clean up the mess before I could continue. As I was cleaning up, my mother explained why smothering the fire extinguished it, and why she had not used water.

A short while later, I was given a hand-me-down chemistry set. I was allowed to do the experiments outside, near the kitchen window, at a table my grandfather found for me, but only when my mother was cooking dinner. The alcohol lamp was kept on a fire-resistant tile on the table, and a bucket of water sat near me. No combustible materials were allowed around my workspace, which meant I had to rake up all the leaves around the table. Finally, I had to wear safety clothes—even in the summer, my legs had to be covered in case a chemical spilled. It was great fun watching things bubble, precipitate, or change colors in predictable ways. When I was older, I read about making plastic. I saved my allowance, and the money I made selling empty beer bottles, to buy the necessary materials for making plastic. I was successful—I made free-form buttons! I learned about acids and bases and bought litmus paper and tested all the liquids in the house. I neutralized my mother's leftover morning coffee and lemon juice with diluted solutions of ammonia or soap.

The fact is, I was always trying to figure out how things worked. I loved the feeling I got when I discovered something new. I remember being told by a visitor, after I had shared an observation, that "curiosity killed the cat," to which my mom then replied, "Yes, but satisfaction brought him back." My parents never told me what I was doing was silly or a waste of time. They simply encouraged me by being there to share my wonder. My siblings, in contrast, would give me grief about my "work" and "experiments," but if someone outside my family said anything negative about my work, they were the first to defend my interests.

My parents allowed me to join the Brownies and, later, the Girl Scouts. They supported me in all school-based and educational activities. But the caveat was that this was *my* activity, not theirs. While they provided the basics for my participation in activities—for example, a Brownies uniform and a clarinet—it was my responsibility to pay for the extras like Brownies dues and reeds. To buy the extras, my sisters and I collected empty beer and soda bottles. Quart beer and soda bottles were the best, because each was worth five cents, whereas six- and twelve-ounce soda bottles were worth two and three cents, respectively. I learned to add, multiply, and divide at an early age, because I had to know how much money we should get in total, and how much my share was. By the time I could cash the bottles myself, my older sisters were too embarrassed to exchange the bottles for money, so I became the "hired" exchanger. Depending on my bargaining powers, I earned one or two cents for each bottle I exchanged for them.

On Sundays we received an allowance from my grandfather. At some point, my older sister managed to convince me that it made sense for each of us to get two coins. I got a quarter and a nickel, and my two sisters each took a quarter and a dime. On one trip to the store with my older sister, I noticed that she could buy one more candy bar than I could. I protested first to her and then to my parents. When they asked me how much I should get, I went to work and figured out that we should each get thirty-three and one-third cents per week. They then asked me how that could work and where would the one-third of a cent come from? After that discussion, every third Sunday I was given thirty-four cents instead of thirty-three.

My parents encouraged me not only to develop and use my math skills in school but also to determine my share of things, figure out interest rates, alter crocheting and sewing patterns, expand and contract recipes, and build things with wood. My parents required us to save five cents from our allowance, and encouraged us to tithe five cents to the church. Most of the gift money that uncles, aunts, and other relatives gave us was deposited in the bank. We each had a savings account. On hearing a bank advertisement that offered higher interest rates on savings accounts than the rate my bank was paying, I told my mother I wanted to move my money to a different bank. She asked me to show her it was worth the trouble. It took me what seemed like hours, but I figured out how much more money I would have after ten years if I were to switch banks. A few days later, my mother and I moved my money. When asked by the teller why I was withdrawing all of my money, I told her I was getting a better inter-est rate at the bank down the street. She laughed, but my mother defended me and verified the reason. My mother then treated me to lunch, which included a root beer float at a drugstore lunch counter. It was a grand day for me!

Beyond the Home Front

There were only two places I could go without supervision when I was eight: Don Jose's, and the library. Don José, the owner of the local liquor store and quick market, had a large family; my mother always pointed out that his daughters went to college and that one was a teacher. Every time we walked past their wraparound porch or drove past their daughter's house in Ganesha Hills, an upscale neighborhood in an adjacent city, my mother would explain how education had made the difference in their lives.

My visits to the library began when I was six or seven. We did not own many books, but my mother made sure we all used the library. I loved the smell of books, their cool pages, and their pictures. The library was always cool in the summer, and the librarians were helpful. During one of my visits, the librarian asked me what I wanted to be when I grew up. My older sister, Rose, was taking physics and loved it. On the front panel of the librarian's desk was a poster of Einstein. I told the librarian I wanted to be like him! She laughed and then said, "You can be a scientist, but you will have to work hard and go to college." I don't remember her name, but I do recall that she would let me check out books even if I owed a few overdue fines. If I could not pay the fines because I had too many, she encouraged me to read the book in the library, and she would help me sound out the words. Eventually, she would let me check books out again. I don't know if my mother paid my fines or if the librarian just wrote them off, but I do remember how happy I was to take out books again. Through reading, I could cook anything, learn anything, go anywhere, and be anyone. I still get great pleasure from reading, and from letting the authors take me to faraway places.

My parents encouraged questions and questioning everything, except their decisions about their children. The worst thing you could be was *tapada* (naive) or *una buena cristiana* (someone who follows without thinking). I remember coming home from fourth grade with California history under my belt. It became a dinner topic when I informed my parents about the evil Spanish and Mexican Californios. My mother and father told me that several of the Californio families were my grandfather's friends, who had had their property taken from them unfairly by the American justice system. Later, in seventh grade, I came home again with patriotic fervor. Our student teacher shared stories of her year abroad in Germany. She described the concentration camps and began to cry. This happened in about 1962 or so, when the memory of the war was still fresh in her mind. After a while she composed herself and told us how the United States had saved the world from this terrible evil. At home, over dinner, I asked my dad why he was not a U.S. citizen, and what he had done to save the world from the Nazis. My dad is very hard of hearing, so he was not accepted into the military. He explained that his laborers' transport truck was conscripted for the war effort. He transported German POWs to the fields where they worked. I asked if he was afraid of the prisoners. "No," he said, "they were young men who were fighting loyally for their government. It was not their fault they were on the wrong side." Then he proceeded to tell me about the Japanese internment camps during World War II, a part of U.S. history that had not been discussed in our World War II lessons. "As long as you look different, some people will not accept you as an American," he said. During my childhood, there was the history we learned in school and church, and the one we learned at home, which often provided further explanation and context.

My parents tried to protect us from the dangers outside of our home, and for the most part they were successful. An immigrant family with eight or nine children moved into a small two-bedroom home across the street from us. This family left each year for *la pizca* (migrant farmwork) after the school year ended, and returned right before the school year started. The children in that family were closer in age to my older brother and sisters. When they returned, they told my siblings about their great adventures—dates, dances at the labor camps, and how much money they had earned.

Tony and Rose, my older siblings, began to lobby my parents for the opportunity to experience *la pizca.* My dad had been a labor contractor from 1938 to 1952 (except during the war years). Neither of my parents understood why their children wanted to work in the fields, because *la pizca* was terribly hard work in the hot sun, with little compensation. Eventually my parents relented (*para que no les salgan granos*) and let us become farmworkers. We packed the car with everything my mother needed to set up housekeeping in a farm-labor camp. We spent our first night in a hotel. The girls slept together, and my dad and brother slept in another room. Our room was big, with a flashing green-and-red neon light outside the window. It was like Christmas. My dad hired us out to pick grapes. We each had a curved knife. Mine was little, because I was only five or six at the time, and I remember my mother telling my dad she hoped I would return with all of my fingers. They wanted me to experience being a farmworker, too.

We woke up early, drove to the vineyard, and waited for first light. We did piecework, so we had to fill as many boxes as possible, as quickly as possible. I think I ate more grapes than I put into the tray that first day. At one o'clock, the boss told us to go home because all the rows had been picked. We went to our "house" in the farm laborers' camp, and the cleaning began. My mother brought out rags, brooms, and mops. We washed every surface with either bleach or Hexol. We took the mattresses outside and beat them, and my mother looked for evidence of bedbugs. She found none, so we wiped the mattresses down with disinfectant, and left them in the sun to dry. By evening the mattresses were dry, but we reeked of Hexol.

The next morning we were in the field again. At the end of that day, we were ready to go home. Farmwork was hot and dirty, there were no toilets, and there were spiders and bees on the grapes. My dad talked to us about being farmworkers: "When you do not want to apply yourselves to your studies, I want you to remember the heat, dirt, bees, spiders, and the low pay. This is the kind of life you can expect if you do not get an education." After a few days of hard, hot work, my dad drove us to Sequoia National Park for a real vacation. We stayed in a rustic log cabin made of dark redwood. My mother still insisted on washing down the toilet and shower before letting any of us use it. While we were on vacation, my dad reminded us of how lucky we were to be able to take advantage of this beautiful spot just a few miles from the labor camp. The people in the labor camp might never have this opportunity, because they did not earn enough money to enjoy the wonders of nature that were so close by.

School Names and Home Names

It is easy to understand why my mother cried when she dropped us off on our first day at school. She held on to her children for as long as she could, because she was unsure what might happen to us in school. My parents understood the value of education because they had been denied access to education. They were also acutely aware of the changes that could come with education. Education challenges the individual and her beliefs. Teachers convey information not only on academic subjects but also on cultural norms. Education socializes youngsters to be "functional" members of the dominant culture. Education changes children. Would we become ashamed of our *mestizo* ethnicity, would we stop eating our traditional foods, would we stop speaking Spanish, or would we become disrespectful of our elders and heritage? Yet with all the potential conflict that education might bring, education was highly valued by my family. My dad would tell me, "You can lose everything you own, but what you know is yours and yours alone. Learn as much as you can."

The genesis of our conflict with education began with the educational system of La Verne, California, the former orange capital of Southern California. La Verne had also been a Ku Klux Klan stronghold. The mantra "separate and unequal" operated in my hometown until after World War II. My parents had attended the "Mexican" school, Palomares Grammar School.

The Palomares School was closed soon after World War II. Before that, Mexican American children had sometimes been allowed to attend the "regular" school as long as they were not Catholic, another group hated by the KKK. But now all the "Mexicans" from our neighborhood were permitted to attend Lincoln School, the "white" school. It struck me as ironic that the whites-only school was named after President Lincoln, a leader associated with racial equality. My cousin was among the first Catholic Mexican Americans to attend the "white" school. My aunt, Pauline Zavala, was a prime mover in this effort. She could see that the kids who went to Palomares never went to high school, much less college. She would be damned if her kids did not get the education that the "Americans" had. She put her hands on her hips, cocked her head, and said, "*Mira m'ija.* We pay taxes just like them." Lincoln was about a mile away. We had to cross a highway and walk through the white neighborhoods, where it was sometimes made clear that we were not welcome. Oddly enough, there had been bus service for school-age kids in my neighborhood when the white orchard owners lived adjacent to our neighborhood. However, after the orange groves were sold and the owners and their families had moved away, the buses stopped running to my neighborhood. Obviously, there were no more children who needed bus rides to school.

The integration of Lincoln School was still relatively recent when I entered kindergarten in 1955. The school was renamed Roynon School, after the administrator who had helped to integrate it. The fact that my Aunt Pauline and other Mexican American parents had pressed Mr. Roynon for these changes had been "forgotten." My aunt and her *comadres* were able to effect this change because of a California Supreme Court decision that helped to set the stage for *Brown v. Board of Education*. In addition, when the Chicano GIs returned from World War II and the Korean War, they were able to go to college. There was concern that one or more of them might notice the separate and unequal education available, and things might get out of hand if the children of these war heroes were denied access to the white school.

The integration of "Mexicans" into the school meant we had to make changes to our names. My mother gave us "school names." We also had our "home names" and, of course, everyone had a street name—Chata, Flaca, Sixes, Snake, Tomate. A few weeks before I went to school, my mother gave me my school name, Mary Ellen. I used that name until late in my senior year of college, and ever since I have used María Elena. Why did we have to change our names? It was part of the assimilation model that the school imposed. My mother was also concerned that we would be ignored or mistreated if we were perceived as recently arrived Mexicans. Using school names would assure the teachers that we were Mexican *Americans.*

The process of our Americanization occurred in the classroom and on the playground. Spanish was not allowed to be spoken on the school grounds or in the classroom. We were sitting around the rug in kindergarten one day, singing and being happy. My new friend, Carmi, raised her hand. She needed to use the toilet, but all she could say was "*Baño,* please." The teacher ignored her, then told her to use the right word. We wanted to help her, but the teacher insisted Carmi say it herself. She started crying, and the next thing we knew there was a puddle on the floor. Carmi had peed in her pants. She stood by the door in her wet clothes for the rest of the day. After that day no one forgot how to say *toilet* again.

"You Are Mexican and You Can Read"

My first-grade teacher, Mrs. Brown, had brown "nurse's" shoes, huge breasts that rivaled my great-grandmother's, kind eyes, and hair sitting like a brown bowl on her head. After a few weeks in school, she sorted us into reading groups. As I walked to line up for recess, she bent down and told me, "You are Mexican and you can read." That afternoon I announced to my mother that I was Mexican and I could read. I was filled with pride. My mother was sewing, and without looking up said, "Well, everyone in your family is Mexican and we all read. Mexicans are supposed to read." My father, grandfather, and great-grandparents told me stories about the lives of great leaders and readers in Mexico. My parents countered racist comments not with anger but by showing me how wrong even teachers could be. At a very early age, I learned to accept that two or more truths could exist at the same time. My parents also made it clear that we could see things from a different perspective. The teachers were not wrong; they just did not know any better, but they deserved to be respected for their position, if not their knowledge. My parents empowered me to question everything and seek my own truths.

Speaking Spanish in school merited the worst punishment delivered on the playground—sitting on the double yellow line. A double yellow line painted on the black asphalt was the demarcation between playground and classroom. Children being punished had to sit on the double yellow line on the hot asphalt in the sun, and their classmates could mock and taunt them. The double yellow line was reserved for those who committed heinous schoolyard crimes, such as intentionally pushing someone to the ground, hitting someone with a closed fist, or speaking Spanish. At play on the schoolyard, Spanish brought many Mexican American children the ultimate punishment. *"Dame la pelota"* (give me the ball) was shouted in the heat of the moment during a game of four-square. The yard-duty teacher, hearing Spanish, would rush over and hiss, "Who said that?" If no one stepped forward, she would ask an Anglo child, who might point to the culprit. Denials might follow, but usually the offender would be directed to the edge of the playground to the double yellow line.

In general, I did well in school. My success was in part the result of my parents' knowledge of the school system, my older siblings' experiences with teachers and counselors, and my mother's involvement in the PTA and attendance at school board and city council meetings. My father would drive my mother to these meetings and wait in the car, often sleeping, because he worked twelve-hour days. Because of my track placement, there were only one or two other Mexican Americans in my classes. This ultimately meant that most of my friends were Anglos. My best friends in school were the sons and daughters of the professionals in my community; at that time, there were few Chicano professionals.

"Your Kind of People Needs Some Kind of Skill"

Typing remains my handicap. My college-prep schedule in high school included typing, and I knew that assignments in college included typed reports. My older sister, who attended community college, was a skill-ful typist, and I saw how important it was to her academic success. But after a semester of typing class, I could see that she could type and I could not. I was not used to earning a C in any subject, and I decided that it was time to drop the class and add Spanish, the course that all of my college-bound friends were taking.

Changing a yearlong course for another in the middle of the academic year took some planning, so I consulted my sister, Sofía. She knew my counselor and warned me that he might not allow this course change, but if I prepared a written request, he might consider it. During my appointment with the counselor, I explained that I was not successful in typing and had reached a plateau in my perfor-mance. After I finished, he said, "Your kind of people needs some kind of skill." I told him that I was going to be a scientist and that Spanish was a better college-prep course. He laughed dismissively and told me if the Spanish teacher agreed to let me take his class he would sign off. The Spanish teacher, Mr. Dávila, listened to my request; I also told him I was going to college and I wanted to be well prepared. He gave me a tentative approval, as long as I took the Spanish IA final and passed.

My mother had taught us to read and write in Spanish at home, and my older siblings had taken Spanish in high school. For two nights before the exam, Sofía showed me some parallels between Spanish and English grammar, and some tricky verb conjugations. I went in for the exam ill prepared, but with great hope. Two days later, Mr. Dávila gave me the news. I had failed the exam, but my grade was nearly a pass. He looked at me steadily and said, "I'm going to take a chance with you. You will have to work very hard, and I expect your best effort. I will let you into my class." In the end, I earned an A in the class. I never really thanked Mr. Dávila, but his show of confidence made a difference in my life. Unfortunately, I know that the counselor continued to stereotype students until his retirement.

As in grammar school, my high school classmates were mostly white. Henry Gonzáles, Joe Zamudio, and I were the three Chicano constants in the college-bound courses. My parents attended college nights, although they were not too certain about my going away to college. I suppose all the Nancy Drew books I had read made college seem a real possibility to me. Besides, I knew kids who were not in the academic honors society (California Scholarship Federation, or CSF) and did not hold leadership positions, and yet they expected to go to college, so I figured I would be accepted, too. On the day of my graduation and college appointment, I met with the counselor, Mr. Harry.

"What are you doing here?" Mr. Harry asked.

"I'm scheduled to talk about graduation and college today," I replied.

"Well, do you think you'll graduate?" he asked.

He reclined in his chair and put his hands over his belly. "Where do you think you will go? Mount San Antonio College?" he said, referring to the local junior college. At that point I told him I planned on applying to Pomona College, University of California, Los Angeles, University of California, Santa Barbara, La Verne College, and my backup school, University of California, Riverside. Our CSF coordinator had taken us to visit all of the nearby University of California (UC) schools, my friend's father worked at La Verne College, and my boyfriend attended Pomona College, so I knew about those schools and explained my choices.

"How do you expect to get into Pomona, the UC schools, or La Verne without a good GPA and SAT scores? You may not have a chance," he said bluntly. I stood my ground and requested the catalogs, applications, and financial aid forms, if he had them. He then said with a chuckle, "Well, if you think you can apply to Pomona, then you should apply to Stanford, too. Not that you'll get into either." By that time it was clear to me that he had not looked at my file. I was about to give up. I gathered my books and walked out. I was nearly in tears when one of the secretaries in the office, who had overheard the exchange, said, "You apply. Here are the things you need." I later discovered I was third in my high school class of nearly three hundred students, which was a surprise to me, based on the counselor's assessment. I was accepted to all of the colleges I applied to.

What Does a Chicana Botanist Look Like?

My daughter and I talk about clothes. She likes to dress up, while I do it only under duress. It makes me feel like I am dressing to gain approval or to "fit the part." Not that I don't like nice fabrics! Beautifully woven, long-staple cottons, silks, and cashmeres feel fabulous against the skin, and bias-cut clothes flow and hug the body. While I have a closet full of skirts, dresses, and pants, I find the notion that I have to look "right" disturbing. On some level, I can never look "right" as the first Chicano or Chicana to earn a PhD in botany at the University of California, Berkeley, or the first Chicana PhD botanist in the country. How can I determine how I should look? After all, how does a Chicana botanist look? My botanist models were always whites (Anglos) and mostly male. Not fitting into either of these categories has allowed me a significant amount of freedom. I have taken it upon myself to determine how I should look. The results have been a bit risky and have caused me a few difficult moments in my professional life.

While I lived in my parents' home, I was taught and expected to dress appropriately. In part, my mother wanted us to look nice because she was concerned we might be ridiculed or not served in town if we were poorly dressed. Not "dressing the part" has indeed caused me some trouble as a professional—for instance, when a secretary did not

43

think I could be the Dr. Zavala who had an appointment with the vice president in charge of computing. Another time, I was denied a pass for faculty parking because I did not "look" like a faculty member. And on another occasion, after telling another parent at my daughter's preschool that I worked at the university, I was asked which offices I cleaned.

I still prefer jeans, a simple shirt, and sandals or sneakers to slacks, suits, dresses, panty hose, and leather shoes. When I became the president of the Society for the Advancement of Chicanos and Native Americans in Science, I had to buy a few dresses, suits, and skirts because I was no longer representing only myself, but also the many Chicana/o and Native American scientists in the United States. I modified the "professional uniform" by including Mexican or Indian jewelry or by adding a *rebozo.* These accessories were a positive reminder of why I tolerated the dress-up clothes, cold weather, bad food, and missing my family. If clothes make the woman, I think they have certainly made the Chicana botanist that I am—comfortable in my skin and in my jeans.

College and Beyond

College was such a different experience from high school. First, I was amazed that I was in college. So many books, so much to learn! The professors at Pomona College were challenging and supportive. It was a great place to think new thoughts and try new ideas. Most of my peers were financially well off compared to me, but that did not matter. What mattered was the thinking and learning. One of the best moments of my undergraduate years was when I was given a key to the botany library. I read whatever caught my fancy. *Curtis Magazine* particularly impressed me, with its beautiful botanical illustrations. It was wonderful going into the library stacks and feasting on the books on flowers. It also amazed me to learn that scientists were still writing about their discoveries in scientific journals. When I had seen *Scientific American* in my library in my hometown, it had seemed like a text to me. But in this library, there were journals with brand-new science. How amazing!

In one plant physiology class, we were assigned to write summaries and evaluations of journal articles. At the beginning, it took hours to read even the shortest of articles, but eventually I learned how to dissect the readings. Because the authors try to convince readers of their "truths," using the results of their experiments to test the hypotheses, and because the articles are jargon-ridden, reading scientific literature takes practice. This type of reading stood in sharp contrast to reading a textbook, where the facts are supposed to be accurate and, in general, are accepted by the student. The question was, would scientists publish errors? If they did, then how would I know this? Reading journal articles was my first formal training in critical thinking.

One of the best features of my major, botany, was the extended weekend field trips we took. In the fall, the trips were to national parks in the Southwest, where the emphasis was on the biogeography, ecology, and geology of the area. In the spring, the field trips focused on increasing our plant collections. We would hike and hunt for plants all day, and key them out at night. It never ceased to amaze me how my botany professors, Drs. Benson and Phillips, were always ready to help us, their enthusiasm never waning.

Our advanced courses included capstone exercises, which required devising a question and a hypothesis, and then creating an experiment to test that hypothesis. These exercises were challenging because you had to learn to ask a well-formed question, which meant reading journal articles, and you would not know if you would get the expected result until the experiment was completed. The important lesson we learned from these exercises was that a "failed" experiment meant you had done the wrong experiment (then you were required to devise another experiment that might work), or that you had asked the wrong question; in any case, your experiment had not really failed, provided you learned something about the system. Our professors were brimming with information and interesting perspectives on approaches in science; they also guided by inquiry, and gave us the freedom to become immersed in topics that were important to us.

As a sophomore, I could hardly believe it when my fellow students quit their studies to protest the Vietnam War. I, too, opposed the war, and would join Dr. Hamilton, a math professor, on Fridays for a silent peace vigil. But I could not understand why the students did not protest the social injustices that were going on in Claremont, where we went to school. A street in town was to be widened without consideration of the Mexican American children or families who lived on the other side of the new four-lane roadway. The children from the neighborhood would have to cross this wide road to walk to school or town. I knew about the road construction because my mother's cousin lived on the "wrong" side of the widened street. A similar access controversy arose in my hometown, but my mother protested and proved that there were children in our neighborhood attending Roynon School. Either a light would need to be installed at a very busy intersection, or bus service would need to be provided. She single-handedly canvassed each house and gave a block-by-block tally of the distribution of children in the neighborhood. These data were presented to the school board and city planners. My mom successfully got the light installed *and* school bus service reestablished.

In another instance, La Verne College wanted to close a street that provided access to another part of the barrio. The problem was that most of the people who used the street walked, and their weight did not trip the meter. My mother requested another study of the use of the street. She found out when the meter was running, and asked all of the people in the neighborhood to drive their parents and grand-parents to town rather than allowing them to walk to town. I think that all of the Chicanos in La Verne who had a car went up and down that street several times when the meter was in place. My parents did not believe in weeping and wailing over problems. They believed in thoughtful action. They taught us to be creative problem solvers. To this day, when things seem wrong to me, I take thoughtful action.

Graduate school at the University of California, Berkeley, was different again from my undergraduate education at Pomona. I was not prepared to deal with the competitive nature of graduate studies. There was not much of a cooperative spirit, and more of the cutthroat atmosphere I had observed among premed students at Pomona. The graduate students in my department were under pressure to demon-strate their worth as scientists, and this necessity was stressed by senior graduate students who told us at student events, "Remember, you have to prove you are worthy of joining the club." It was ominous.

When I was in my first year of graduate school, I met with Dr. Arturo Madrid, who visited all the Ford Foundation predoctoral fellowship winners at UC Berkeley. I explained that at Pomona it was assumed I could be a scientist, while at Berkeley I had to prove I could be a scientist. I also mentioned the "pissing contests" that were part of the student pecking order and the student evaluation process by faculty. There was also the prevailing notion of "lesser" people at Berkeley, those Berkeley PhDs who went on to work at institutions that were not research intensive. The message was clear that UC Berkeley botany PhD students must be "clones" of their UC Berkeley botany professors.

Sexism was obvious within the botany department, despite the fact that the department, which was among the first to offer a PhD at UC

Berkeley, had a history of awarding women the degree. However, the first woman professor was not hired in the department until the mid-1970s, and ultimately she was not tenured. We were told, "Yes, we produce women PhDs and they are good, but the botany department has to protect itself against 'intellectual inbreeding.'" However, it did not take long to understand that the inbreeding applied only to women, because there were several male faculty members in the department who were alumni.

I remember sitting in a tutorial with my then-mentor when his phone rang. I excused myself but he motioned for me to stay. I heard him describe a woman scientist as a workhorse, but not creative. It shocked me to hear his assessment, because just a few days earlier I had heard him praise her highly for her diligence in getting to the bottom of a sticky systematic problem. His next comment convinced me to change thesis advisors. He told the caller that while he had never heard of the other scientist they were considering, and did not know his work, he would offer the position to the man. I worked hard to find another project, and left my first mentor as soon as I could. Fortunately for the woman, the interviewer must have ignored my mentor's comments, because a few weeks later she came by and informed us at tea that she had accepted the position.

As a graduate student, I decided I did not want to be like most of the professors in my department. At tea one day, a professor said, "When it comes down to it, we are this much space on a shelf." He varied the distance between his hands from a few inches to a foot or so. His observation might not have troubled me so much if the other professors present had countered his claim, but none did. I felt that his vision was an awful way to evaluate the worth of a life and career. One of my PhD mentors, William Jensen, had a life filled with research, family, teaching, and creative activities. He gave his time to us generously and was always willing to talk with us about our experiments—a recent, successful one, or even a failed one. His family life was complex, but he balanced his research, teaching, and service. In an attempt to help "humanize" the faculty for the students, I organized a hobby show, in which members of the faculty and PhD staff shared their outside interests with the department. Most were reluctant, but a few allowed me to display their ceramics, prints, and photos. It encouraged us to know that we might one day have free time again.

My graduate experience was not particularly unusual. Feelings of isolation and doubt are common among graduate students. The transition from someone who learns to someone who generates knowledge is a demanding and rigorous path to undertake. But in my estimation it was a worthwhile one.

While graduate school was difficult, being a postdoc was fun. In general, the people I worked with were gems. They actively engaged me in my development, were fair and honest with me about my strengths, and helped me overcome my weaknesses. All were high-achieving white males. I owe much to Paul Mahlberg, Bernard Finkle, Joseph Corse, and Ian Sussex, who were willing to discuss, defend, and share their insights with me. I put Ian to a real test of patience. He allowed me to stay in his laboratory while I recovered from an airplane accident and a recluse spider bite, mishaps that removed me from active research for over two years. All the while, Ian and his laboratory group let me do what I could without calling my commitment to science into question. Ian developed a community of scholars in his laboratory group. He felt that we should all be able to learn from one another, because we each had a gift to share.

I must admit there have been turning points along my career path that I have not always navigated with grace. I have had to learn to approach transitions carefully. In the past, not being able to handle a transition earned me my first D (in my freshman year), and nearly got me kicked out of graduate school after receiving a C! From those experiences, I learned to watch for the unwritten rules. It was hard to imagine that such rules existed in science. After all, scientists are trained to be fair and objective. Shouldn't these attributes carry through to treatment of students and colleagues? Shouldn't the rules be explicit for all to know? It is not enough to be a good scientist—one also has to understand the culture of science. I think understanding this concept is a common hurdle for all first-generation college students, graduate students, and professionals. One of the benefits that organizations such as the Society for the Advancement of Chicanos and Native Americans in Science (SACNAS) provide to their members, most of whom are first-generation college students, is an understanding of this culture. The Women in Cell Biology and the minorities affairs committees of some national societies have also provided this type of guidance. One of my responsibilities is to help the next generation of first-generation college students and professionals become aware of the culture of science.

Gifts Come in Many Guises

Choosing a career path is not always easy. From an early age, I knew I would become a scientist, but where I fit in as a scientist was another matter. My academic pedigree had prepared me for a position at a research-intensive university. After completing my PhD at Berkeley, I worked at Indiana University, in Dr. Paul Mahlberg's laboratory, for nearly two years. Then I moved back to Berkeley and worked at the U. S. Department of Agriculture (USDA), where I completed the first reported localization of plant hormone in situ.

While I was between projects at the USDA, I flew to Boston to meet my boyfriend, planning to finish filling out a Ford Foundation postdoctoral fellowship application while there. Unfortunately, our plane did not land safely at Logan Airport. I was in an airplane crash. It was my good fortune that I did not die, because I had intended to change my seat to one near the front of the plane. Our landing in Logan Airport ended in Boston Harbor. The people who died as a result of the crash, the passengers in the row to which I had intended to move, were presumably washed out to sea. After learning this, I decided I was and am living on borrowed time, so I had better make good use of it. From the crash, I suffered knee damage and internal injuries. People still ask me, "How can you fly?" Simply put, if I did not, I could not do my job. The first time I went back to the airport after the crash, I panicked and threw up when I smelled the jet fuel. For months after and even now, when I am under extreme stress, I dream about the plane crash. For a time after the crash, I could walk only with difficulty and could not stand for long periods, not a promising state of affairs for a lab scientist. The internal injuries did not completely manifest themselves for a year. They were then variously misdiagnosed, until at last they were identified correctly. Over a period of nearly three years, there were times when I could not stand, walk, sit, or eat without being in terrible pain. While my postdoc peers were pumping out papers, I was practicing yoga for pain control (or taking drugs when the pain was not controllable), relearning patience, reading broadly, and preparing for a career shift—I was seriously considering a move to the field of medicine. I took courses to complete the premed curriculum and applied to medical schools. But as soon as my SACNAS *tíos* (aunts and uncles) caught wind of my potential career change, I was invited to apply to the Michigan State University (MSU) Rosa Parks/César Chávez Visiting Professor program by Diana Marinez. She and I had worked together previously on a teacher education project for SACNAS.

One of my top medical school choices was Howard University, because it provided a medical education that emphasized interaction with patients with chronic diseases, such as diabetes and hypertension. I was accepted at Howard, and a few days later I was also offered the Rosa Parks/César Chávez visiting professorship at MSU. I was torn. I took long walks in the country, made plus-and-minus lists, talked with my boyfriend (and future husband), and prayed. In the end, I determined that while most of the people I wanted to work with suffer "poverty" illnesses (hypertension, stress, and obesity), I could not fix poverty as a physician. I could, on the other hand, see that my education had positively influenced my younger siblings and nieces and nephews, so I concluded I could accomplish more good for my people as a professor than as a physician. I decided to decline the acceptance to Howard and accept the offer from MSU.

In 1980, I went to my first SACNAS conference, in Albuquerque. It was a completely amazing event. I had never seen so many Chicano and Native American scientists gathered in one room. Even though there were only two hundred of us at the meeting, the presence of these successful, respected scientists made me feel very proud. After the sessions, we met at the bar. I listened to the jokes being told— they were like the ones my mother would not let me hear when my uncles came over for parties! That's when SACNAS became my scientific family. I met a number of Chicanos and Native Americans at that meeting who have helped me along my way since then. I have taken the liberty of asking them for advice and to serve on committees, and I have helped them when asked. I have SACNAS *tíos* and SACNAS *hermanos*, and now some SACNAS nieces and nephews. I know that my SACNAS *tíos* have looked after me, and I wonder what might have become of me if they had not extended a hand even before I knew I needed one. When I was offered a position at California State University, Northridge (CSUN), at the same time that I was being considered for a tenure-track position at MSU, and my SACNAS *tíos* heard I would accept the position at CSUN, my phone started ringing. They asked if my marriage was falling apart, whether I was having a midlife crisis, or if I had suffered a nervous breakdown and was in need of counseling. How else could I explain "throwing away" my excellent research training and end up "just" teaching? I was not playing the game according to the tier-one script.

How did I get myself into this position? I was named the Rosa Parks/César Chávez Visiting Professor at MSU. The program offered an opportunity for the department and the scholar to determine if this was a good fit. I had done the things a first-year tenure-track faculty member is supposed to do: I had been awarded a significant National Science Foundation (NSF) starter grant, my teaching evaluation was good, a paper was in press, and I was known as a good colleague. However, my mentor in the biochemistry department counseled me that to stay at MSU I would need an offer from another university. I thought, "that seems really stupid," but I knew I had to play the game and sought the other offer.

A few days later, I received a phone call from Dr. Warren Furumoto at CSUN. He described the "target of opportunity" program at CSUN and invited me to visit. To be perfectly honest, I really loved working at MSU. My colleagues were a welcoming, friendly group of hardworking but fun-loving, more or less balanced scientists. The scientific opportunities for collaboration were excellent, and there was opportunity for advancement. My husband and I had purchased a house, and we were imagining ourselves raising children in Michigan. Although I accepted the invitation to CSUN, I viewed it only as a bargaining chip.

But what I saw at CSUN was a school with potential; the students were incredibly hardworking and hungry for an education, but the university had few resources to help them develop that promise. I also saw that there were only four plant biologists at CSUN, while there were over one hundred twenty at MSU. I saw the possible end of my research-driven scientific career and the beginning of another career that, while still including research, would focus on developing human capital, and, in particular, minority human capital in the sciences. The laboratory space at CSUN was minor compared to what I had at MSU, the teaching load was twelve times greater, the housing was four times more expensive in Northridge than in East Lansing, and the pay was only one-third more. It was no wonder my SACNAS *tíos* thought I had lost my mind altogether. But in my socially responsible, daughter-of-my-parents heart of hearts, I knew I had to do what I could to ensure equitable access to high-quality education to California students whose families were like mine.

The chance to help students led me to choose CSUN. I felt I might make a real difference at CSUN, and to date I think I have. There are some downsides to working there. It has taken some time to change the culture to one that acknowledges and values how important it is for faculty to be engaged in research with students to provide an up-to-date, well-trained, technologically savvy workforce. It is harder to get grant proposals funded when they are proposed by CSUN, and harder to get papers published when you are not at a research-intensive university. However, the upside for me is considerable: I am only fifty-five miles from my parents' home and from my extended family, and my colleagues are hardworking, well-trained, bright people who enjoy working with students and who have happy, healthy families and other interests in addition to their work.

Moving to Northridge shifted my priorities, but the earthquake of 1994 totally realigned them. I had been awarded a grant based on the existence of biological reagents we had made with the support from an NSF grant. However, after the earthquake, laboratory freezers thawed, and cell storage tanks filled with liquid nitrogen reached ambient temperature. All our cell lines, antibodies, and reagents were spoiled. As the program director of the Minority Access to Research Careers (MARC) and brand-new CSUN Minority Biomedical Research Support (MBRS) programs, which had been funded in October 1993 (the earthquake struck on January 17, 1994), I contacted the National Institutes of Health (NIH) to discuss our status, and was informed that if we could not show a commitment from the university to get the laboratories back in order and running, our awards would be discontinued. Such action would have cut the research support for five or six faculty members, and all research opportunities and financial support for the students in the MARC and MBRS programs. I called the president's office, which was temporarily housed in a tent on a rain-soaked lawn, and explained the grant situation to her. I wrote a letter of commitment for the president, which she signed, and the NIH did not cut our funding. When a SACNAS *tío* in Washington DC heard that all our unique reagents were lost, he recommended I leave CSUN before my scientific reputation was ruined. My husband and I chose to stay.

I have had many mentors in my life, even before I knew what one was. I think those who had the greatest positive influence on me as I moved along my path were my parents, my siblings, my grandfather Donicio, and my great-grandparents. My husband and daughter are also "partners in crime." There were many teachers who said the right things at the right times to encourage me, and other teachers who said the wrong things, but whose words spurred me on to show them differently. During the moments when I needed someone to show me the ropes, that person has always managed to come along and then graciously leave, allowing me the freedom to choose my rope and swing as far as I wanted.

I met my husband, Jim Parker, when we were both postdocs at Yale. He was looking for a room, and I had a spare room to rent.

While he did not like the room, he did like the apartment's occupant. Today we are best friends, and although we have a mixed marriage— he is a social scientist and I am a natural scientist!—we are politically very closely aligned. We have a wonderful daughter, Daniela, who as a baby was often cared for, when I had to travel for meetings and conferences, by my younger sister, Christina. Two of my nieces, Amelia and Angélica, have also been companions to my daughter. My husband and daughter have brought new dimension to my life, and my career accomplishments are due in part to their support, understanding, and willingness to share their partner and mother with others.

What is my legacy? My legacy lies in three areas: home, career, and community service. My daughter is growing up to be a confident, kind, well-spoken person, and she is a highlight of my life. My husband and I have a caring, loving relationship, which is also important to me. Although I have accumulated few research publications, one of my articles that is now over twenty-two years old is still cited. So maybe that Berkeley professor was correct, maybe a scientist occupies only so much space on a shelf. However, a major focus of my scientific career has been my work with students. I have worked with hundreds of students at CSUN, many of them members of underrepresented minority groups in science. Before I arrived at Northridge, the number of minority students who entered PhD programs after graduating from CSUN was extremely low. When I graduated from Pomona College, about 70 percent of the graduating class entered graduate or professional school. Based on my experiences at Pomona, I have developed programs at CSUN for students who might be interested in entering PhD programs in basic and biomedical sciences. Funded by the National Institutes of Health General Medicine, these programs have provided long-term support to our university, which has enabled us to make a difference in young people's life choices. Many minority students do not know what their career options are as high-achieving science students. Often, the only professionals they and their families are aware of are medical doctors, dentists, veterinarians, and nurses. The success of our program participants, who have earned doctoral degrees from some of the top PhD programs in the country, demonstrates that minority students are interested in and capable of becoming full participants in developing new knowledge. To succeed, they must be given the support that allows them to develop research skills, a strong fundamental knowledge in their field of study, and freedom from significant financial hardship. Our country must respond to the needs of our young people regarding access to high-quality education. If policy makers continue to ignore the development of over 25 percent of our country's population (Chicanos/Latinos, African Americans, and Native Americans), the future of this country is bleak. We will lose our competitive edge in all areas that require a highly skilled, creative, well-educated workforce. With the loss of our competitive edge in science and technology, we are primed to lose our status in the world's economy.

Replenishing

Allowing time for my interests outside of science has made me a more balanced, happier person. I enjoy music, family, eating, cooking, and reading. I have practiced yoga off and on for nearly twenty-five years, which I find is the most intense and practical way of relaxing. I still enjoy hiking in the Sierra Nevada, and look forward to the time when my daughter and I can do an overnight backpacking trip. I enjoy the company of friends and attending college basketball games. I enjoy going to museums and plays, and I have played several instruments, including the clarinet and the bassoon. I enjoy creating with my hands—sewing, knitting, crocheting, and stitching. Cooking is also satisfying because the results are nearly instantaneous, unlike weeklong or monthlong projects. It is very sensual to cook. The smell, colors, and feel of the foods are marvelous, and when a recipe of my own devising is extremely appetizing, it is satisfying to share my culinary treats. Before the plane crash, I ran 10K races and would often run twenty-five to thirty-three miles a week, but now I use the cross-trainers at the gym to get into that very special inner space. I miss the air on my face and the outdoor environment, but the overall pleasure and benefit of exercise is the same.

My family, my colleagues, my students, my mentors, my SACNAS family, and most of all my love of science—all are gifts that have enriched my life and shaped who I am. I truly believe I am more than a space on a shelf.

CHAPTER 3

Life Lessons

Cleopatria Martínez
Professor of Mathematics

I was born in Las Vegas, New Mexico. My mother had only a third-grade education, but my father and his two siblings were schoolteachers in Canjilon, New Mexico, which is why I later considered teaching as a profession. My parents separated when I was three years of age, and my mother brought us to Denver, Colorado, where she had a sister. I did not see my father again until I was twelve, when Mom took me to his funeral; he had died in a car accident. I grew up with my mom, my grandmother (who spoke only Spanish), a younger brother, and a sister. Mom did not receive child support, and her limited education kept her from getting a well-paying job, so we were forced to go on welfare and live in the Quigg Newton housing projects of north Denver. Each month Mom received a ninety-dollar welfare check, half of which went to pay our rent. Mom became an excellent seamstress and often bought adult clothing at the local Goodwill Store, which she would painstakingly take apart, cut, and resew to fit our little bodies. I did not wear a new store-bought dress until I was fourteen years old.

When I started kindergarten, I spoke only Spanish, was dark-skinned, had two braids with my hair parted in the middle, and wore clothes from the Goodwill Store. I was ashamed of these things until I stopped listening to "society." Ultimately, my life of poverty, discrimination, and

Cleopatria Martínez with her brother Bob, 1953.

shame–combined with my mom's *dichos* and her love of knowledge– became the foundation of my motivation to get a PhD.

As children, my siblings and I had little money and therefore no toys or balls to play with, so we learned to make do with whatever was available and became quite inventive. For entertainment we climbed Dumpsters and one- or two-story buildings. Sometimes I walked on or twirled around the tops of the steel bars used for the chain-link fences that bordered the projects. Once we wrapped an old shirt around some bundled material to form a ball, to which we tied a found rope, forming an adequate tetherball. I was competitive and, like everyone else, wanted to win, so I studied the flight and speed of the "tetherball." I soon discovered that the best path was when the ball was too high for my opponent to reach. If I stood 180 degrees across from my opponent, the tetherball's flight would come to its lowest point where I was standing, allowing me to comfortably reach it and control its path.

In high school I used my childhood experiences to help me excel on the girls' gymnastics team. For example, the balance beam had a flat four-inch surface, which was much easier to walk on than the rounded, two-inch-diameter steel bars to which I was accustomed. It was also easier to twirl around the uneven parallel bars because they were made of wood, unlike the steel bars of the projects. My outdoor play experiences with movement, height, balance, and spinning helped me greatly when learning the many tumbling and twirling activities of the floor exercise, balance beam, and uneven parallel bars. In gymnastic stunts, the body moves through distinct paths, such as the parabolic and circular paths, that are described by mathematical formulas. To successfully perform many gymnastic stunts, the gymnast must be aware of the points of release during a spin for either maximum height or to create a direction of linear movement. These points of release can be found in equations of mathematical tangent lines. It is a thrilling experience when you release at the perfect moment in time and your body follows the right path, allowing you to land balanced on your feet. It is also exciting to work the mathematics that describes this physical movement. If there is movement, then there is mathematics. As I like to tell my students, "Math is all around you."

Significant Events: School and Schooling

My mother's dictum, "No matter what you do in life, always do your best," followed me everywhere and has helped shape my life. Even if I were to become a ditch digger, I would try to be the best ditch digger around. Her advice was in response to people calling Mexicans "lazy." She observed, "Mexicans are some of the hardest-working people doing jobs that no one else wants." Consequently, as I considered going to college, I researched what "best" meant in academic terms and discovered a PhD was the best degree you could attain in education. That is how my educational goal in life was set.

I studied diligently, and as a result of my hard work, I became an A student in school, but I still had no clue as to what I was going to be when I grew up. I was hoping it would just occur to me—I thought I would eventually "see the light." But such a revelation did not happen. Like a detective, I began problem solving, trying to figure out the parameters of my likes and dislikes. An assignment in my junior high English class helped me see the direction I should follow. To my delight, my English teacher gave us the freedom to write about any subject we chose, her sole stipulation being that the topic be interesting. I wrote about the most interesting topic I could think of at that time and proudly handed in my essay. When I received a poor grade, I was so traumatized that to this day I cannot remember the topic I wrote about. I had never questioned the teacher's judgment before, but I had to ask why I had gotten such a low grade. My teacher's response was that the essay "was simply not interesting." I could not understand how something I found so interesting could be considered completely uninteresting to this teacher. After considerable thought, I realized the tremendous subjectivity of the assignment: I had written the essay from my point of view, not the teacher's. In my excitement over the perceived freedom of the assignment, it had not occurred to me that the awarded grade would be dependent on what the teacher considered interesting.

While I believe education should be an objective activity, I have had to conclude that it is not. During the completion of my coursework on my PhD, I tested this theory again. The professor assigned a book that contained the "most innovative ideas" for developing school schedules. Our assignment was to create a totally innovative school schedule, using ideas presented in our text. I asked myself, "Does he really want an innovative schedule, or is he actually a traditional educator?" I wrote three versions: a truly innovative schedule, a partially innovative schedule, and a completely traditional schedule. Before the due date, I handed in the schedule in which I incorporated many of the author's recommended innovations as a draft for feedback from the professor. He did not find the schedule innovative and commented on the weakest sections, which were actually verbatim implementations of the textbook author's innovations. I then showed the professor the partially innovative version, which he said was much better, and ultimately I handed in the most traditional version as my final paper, for which I received an A. That is how I came to conclude that I preferred assignments I could complete without identifying a teacher's likes and dislikes. Obviously, the study of mathematics fits this criterion, since the correct answer is always independent of a teacher's opinion.

Surviving in the Belly of the Beast

I always tried to be optimistic and see the good in each experience. I remember the first time Mom bought a new blanket—not a used one from the Goodwill Store. My brother, sister, and I went to our bed, spread the blanket out and lay under it, pulled it up caressingly to our necks, and said, "luxury, luxury, luxury" over and over again, because we felt we were drenched in luxury like rich people. I was rich with good feelings. I felt drenched in luxury with so little. In experiencing this "richness," I realized the only way for me to achieve a life of "luxury" was to complete my education.

Since my mother had only a third-grade education, I did my homework by myself, which meant I had to read my math textbooks to understand the math. Someone once said, "If you can read mathematics, you can read anything." I frequently came across sentences I did not understand in my math text, and I would read them again and again. Eventually I understood the concept, but I was upset about the time it took to understand the sentence, so I would try to rephrase it in a shorter way. I was surprised to find there was no briefer way of stating the concept. There was a certain beauty to its conciseness. So grew my admiration for mathematics. However, conciseness in language does not necessarily facilitate understanding of concepts. I discovered and prefer having concepts articulated using language the average public comprehends.

As I mentioned, my math homework often took me a long time to complete because I had to reread passages several times; I had to concentrate at each step to avoid introducing an error, which of course would give me the wrong answer. This situation created a problem for me at home, because my brother, sister, and I had assigned chores, and I did not always have enough time to do my chores and my homework. One day, I decided to confront the problem and let my mom know I could not do the dishes because I had too much homework that night. She knew she could not help me with my homework; therefore, she helped me by changing the rules of the house to accommodate me. She told my siblings they were to wash the dishes because homework was more important. This tremendous gift of time made it possible for me to succeed academically. Mathematics is a high-maintenance mistress who requires the learner to give her a great deal of time. My mother's compassion and support allowed me to devote the necessary time to understand the math and succeed academically. Mom offered me a great gift, the gift of time.

The central individuals in my life have been the members of my family and my educators. My relatives were hardworking people, trying to survive one day at a time. In school, I felt common, unappreciated, alone, often invisible, and insignificant. I wanted to know where I was going with my life and searched for meaning and purpose. Looking back, there were several reasons I shunned history as a school subject. The study of history was then presented as a series of names and dates to be memorized, as though the events happened in a vacuum devoid of feelings, emotions, and motivation. Latinos had no presence in the history books. I also did not agree with the teachers' support of historical concepts like assimilation (the movement to make everyone European-like) and manifest destiny (the God-given right of the Europeans to "claim" the Native Americans' land). I was unable to reconcile in my mind how taking control of someone's land and killing the original residents was God's will. Which God advocated this? Not mine.

With respect to assimilation, the buzzword at the time, I felt that the concept did not apply to me. As I understood it, educators believed that the cure-all for our educational and societal ills would be if "they" were to assimilate. I realized the "they" included me and other dark-skinned people. I knew I was not assimilating when I ate the bean-and-tortilla *taquito* for lunch that my mother made instead of the white bread sandwiches the other kids had. Beans and tortillas were inexpensive and affordable. As far as appearances went, I could not change how I looked. I was of Mexican and Indian ancestry, and those were my dominant features. The "American" movement, or my internalized racism, was so effective that when I was a little girl, I wanted to make my skin white, but I could not find the route to whiteness and to assimilation. Additionally, as I grew up I found I was socially more comfortable with people of different cultures than with people of Anglo-Saxon heritage. My closest friends resembled the membership of the United Nations, including girls of Italian, Japanese, Chinese, African American, and Mexican American heritages. Since I did not want everyone to become European-like and surrender their distinctive cultures, I did not support the assimilation movement as a societal cure-all. Later, the slightly more acceptable concept of the United States as a "melting pot" was introduced to promote assimilation. Finally, the idea of a large "salad bowl," which respected cultural differences by leaving them intact, was embraced as the ideal multicultural perspective of the population of the United States.

By mandating assimilation, the educational system was making this little girl crazy. I felt I was an army of one seeing life through the only pair of brown eyes in the room. It was as though I were in the twilight zone, where the teachers agreed with and supported contradictory concepts. I became tired of trying to live according to someone else's beliefs, thoughts, and opinions, tired of trying to become or assimilate into someone I was not. Previously when I worked this hard at a goal, I had always been successful, but I was not able to change myself into the assimilated person my teachers desired. I decided I wanted a career where I could be myself and where my thoughts and ideas were valued. Even today, this is the type of culture I would like the United States to adopt.

The field of mathematics accepted the person I was and proved to be a subject with rules and order. The correct answer was completely objective. I did not need to be blonde and blue-eyed to be successful and appreciated. I did not need to figure out the teacher's likes or dislikes. I was simply expected to solve the problem at hand following established rules, which were equally available to all of us. The rules governing the language of mathematics were stable and fit together neatly. I could always predict the result, and the process made sense along the way. Unlike many other subjects whose facts changed over the years, time did not change the rules of mathematics, and different people solving a problem ended up at the same place. All roads led straight to one answer. This was a delightful change of pace and another reason why I chose a career in mathematics.

In choosing education, I wanted to escape poverty, discrimination, and feelings of not being valuable or worthy. I longed to be liked, accepted, and appreciated for myself, and to have my thoughts, ideas, and opinions respected and valued. The primary sources of power in this country are money, social status, and Anglo-Saxon ancestry. The first two can be improved upon by all people through hard work, education, and tenacity. These qualities are also essential to be success-ful in mathematics. Had I found a way to achieve the respect I yearned for and was sure I deserved? Perhaps.

During my senior year in high school, I actually benefited from the perennial obstacle of poverty. High academic performance and severe poverty won me college scholarships. Ironically, where poverty and being Mexican were traditional indicators of failure, these same attri-butes now helped me get scholarships. The primary obstacle was no longer a lack of money to pay for my education but the fear of losing my identity, heritage, and culture. It seemed to me that everyone who was educated acted superior, a trait I had learned to equate with white people. When I was accepted to Harvard, I feared I would undergo a slow, subtle change and, at the end of my education, would emerge "white." While this fear may seem ridiculous, nearly every educated person I knew until then was white and demonstrated a superior atti-tude toward others. And the very few nonwhite educated individuals in my life acted just as superior as the white people!

While I was in high school I gradually realized I liked my Mexican self and no longer dreamed of being white. In spite of external influ-ences to the contrary, Mom taught me to honor myself, and finally I accepted who I was. Although Mom was green-eyed and fair-skinned and could "pass," she never tried to deceive anyone, because she was proud to be Mexican. Also, she unconditionally loved me, her *negra consentida*, as she lovingly called me. I loved my mother, but I did not like the way society treated her and my grandma, who had very strong Indian features. When I graduated high school, I knew wanting to be white was the same as denying my heritage and my family. I believed I was faced with a dilemma: I could be either poor and uneducated or successful and white. I did not want to wind up at the bottom of the pay scale, but I did not want to relinquish my identity either. While I was convinced that well-paying jobs and success were acquired only by white people, and all educated people were white or acted exactly like white people, I took a deep breath and once again tested fate. I planned to get my college degree and also work hard to maintain my heritage. As it happened, at the end of four years I received a bachelor's degree, and I was honestly astonished that I did not act or believe myself to be superior.

In college, as in public school, I was constantly overcoming stereotypes. I had always been drawn to topics in law, medicine, science, and research, and when I entered my graduate program I had the opportunity to take an educational law class. When I received an A on my first test, the professor asked to see me in his office. He said, "You did very well on the test. Your people don't usually do so well." I was speechless—a state I frequently found myself in following similar comments. While I wanted to let him know how inappropriate this statement was, and perhaps add a few more colorful words, I also wanted to receive my PhD. In the absence of an appropriate response, I fell silent. Now that I have my PhD, few such remarks leave me speechless. I am a proud to be a Chicana from the projects with a PhD.

Truths My Mother Taught Me

Mom worked long hours for very low wages, but she was a hardworking, dependable employee. I learned many virtues from this wonderful person. She was a proud woman who reminded me,

"Never forget where you come from," and "Always do your best." Some people were mean and called us "dirty Mexicans." Mom said, "We may have old, used clothes, but they are always clean and pressed." She was a stickler for cleanliness. Mom affirmed as positive that we were Mexican; she was proud of the fact that we

Cleopatria Martínez with her mother, 2005.

spoke two languages, not just one, and we were always clean. An opposite view of Mexicans was propagated by educators and society. I learned to be neat, accurate, and persistent, to take pride in my work, to do my best, and to do my own learning—the very qualities needed to succeed as a scientist and mathematician.

While education was something Mom was unable to attain for herself, she valued education highly. She often said, "Knowledge is something they can't take away from you." Mom sometimes took us to a nearby farm to pick whatever the farmer was growing. I once asked how much we got paid and found we were paid by the bushel. We worked as fast as we could, and I recorded how long it took us to fill a bushel. I could now compute our pay for a day's work. I discovered that it was humanly impossible to earn enough money to buy anything significant. I realized farmwork was not the way out of poverty, and, more important, I would not be able to leave the world of discrimination unless I earned a great deal of money or was very well educated. There were no wealthy relatives who would mention me in their will and no family business to inherit. Getting out of poverty was up to me alone and education was the key.

Survival Techniques

As I made my way through college and graduate school, I adopted a few survival techniques that helped me through some difficult times. These techniques fell into three categories: 1) the "don't listen to them" solution, 2) look at the issue from a different perspective, and 3) endure the situation, it too shall pass.

"Don't Listen to Them"

Again, it is my wise mother who gave me the skills to disregard some of what others said. My mom did not listen to society's rules, and she often showed us how ridiculous they were. For instance, we were taught there was no such thing as man's work and woman's work. Mom was a single parent and could not afford to be a helpless female. At home she had to do both the "man's job" and the "woman's job." I realize now what a powerful and positive influence she was, because I learned I could do anything. My brother was not exempt from doing the dishes, and my sister and I were not exempt from mowing the grass. Later, I found society's message that mathematics was a man's world equally absurd.

Mom taught us by example to never accept when someone said, "You can't do that!" My mom managed with a third-grade education and no husband. She was made to feel that she would never amount to anything and that her children would be juvenile delinquents. If my mom could get a job, raise three kids, buy a car, get off welfare, rent a house outside the housing projects, and eventually buy a house, imagine what I could do coming from such strong stock! When I was hurt because of some mean-spirited words, my mother would simply say to me, "Don't listen to them." I have found this advice to be one of my most valuable lessons, the one probably most responsible for my success.

A Different Point of View

When I was bombarded with a particularly negative message, I trained myself to look at it from a different point of view. For instance, beginning in elementary school, teachers often presented statistical examples to demonstrate how people like us—poor, Mexican, living on welfare, from a single-parent household—were most likely to fail academically, to experience teenage pregnancy, to go on welfare, and to end up in prison. It was difficult not to take these messages personally or as predictors of my future. I worked hard at not accepting our lifestyle as an indicator of absolute future failure. At these times, I remembered to not listen, or I found something positive to concentrate on. For instance, my teacher showed us the poverty line on an 8½ x 11 paper. She made it sound as though people were barely surviving at the poverty line. I knew we were poor and wondered where my family's income fell with respect to this frightening line, which appeared to mark imminent starvation and death. That evening I asked my mom how much money we earned monthly and found we were so far below the poverty line that we fell at the bottom of the next blank page. Instead of panicking, I rationalized that I would do well to someday reach the poverty line. I chuckled to myself at the absurdity—to have the poverty line as a goal. Looking at things from a different vantage point allowed me to rethink the problem and not necessarily accept it as self-determining. All situations are framed by a particular viewpoint, so why can't I reframe them and act accordingly?

Enduring the Situation

There are times when you cannot find anything positive about the situation. For instance, one day when I was in elementary school my teacher told us we would be taking a field trip and asked each of us to bring a nickel to class the following day. She added, "Everybody has a nickel to spare." She thought it preposterous for someone to not have a nickel. But I knew it was not preposterous; in fact, my mom did not have a nickel for me. I was very embarrassed about how poor we were, and now I felt additionally humiliated by her message. Then the teacher added that if, by some very unusual circumstance, one of us could not bring in a nickel we should notify her. I didn't know what to do. I was too embarrassed to confess we did not have a measly nickel. I never forgot this moment, one of those moments I had to endure. While I could not find anything positive about this experience, I vowed never to embarrass anyone like this, much less a child.

Growing up, I found the school environment quite disingenuous and therefore uncomfortable for me, but that situation propelled me to identify the characteristics of a good teacher and leader. For instance, I did not find the jokes my teachers told to be funny, yet the class laughed. Mom had raised me to be true to myself, so I laughed only when something was truly funny. I considered that perhaps I had a defective sense of humor. Why didn't I see the humor in my teachers' jokes? When I was around my family or other Chicanos, I had a great time and found myself laughing freely because they told some truly funny stories. This at least confirmed that I did have a healthy sense of humor. I concluded that the kids who laughed at the unfunny jokes were brown-nosing the teacher. I, too, liked the way teachers endeared themselves to the popular kids by joking with them, and I wanted to experience that type of interaction. It was never fun watching the teacher's pets get all the attention. The favorites seemed always to be blonde and blue-eyed girls or, if they were brunettes, they were Anglo-Saxon, certainly not someone who wore braids like me. This ruled out any possibility of my becoming a teacher's pet. I learned to endure the situation and not dwell on it. I also determined that teachers should make every child feel like the teacher's pet.

Later, when I was working toward my PhD, I studied bilingual mathematics education, and in one of these classes I encountered my first Latino teacher. I was surprised to see how comfortable the class was for me, because I felt a kinship with the professor, something I had never felt in all my twenty years of education. At long last I found out what comfort in the classroom feels like.

Another unpleasant memory involved the yearly alteration of my name. At the beginning of the school year, when roll was first taken, the teacher would call out each pupil's name. When my name was called, the teacher and the students laughed (which was the same as laughing at me). I suppose the class thought this Spanish-speaking, brown-skinned little girl with braids was not deserving of the name. After that first humiliating day, my name was cut from Cleopatria to Cleo, and I became one of the invisible ones. I now know the correct pronunciation of a person's name shows respect and demonstrates you value them. I am astounded that teachers continue to show disrespect to children by carelessly handling the pronunciation of the student's name. But given the circumstances then, there was little I could do except endure the situation and correct it as soon as I could. Now I proudly use my complete name; Cleo has stayed behind in those insensitive classrooms of my youth.

Celebrations

When I compare my life as a child to the life I have provided for my children, I am aware of the many treasures my mother never knew.

My mother worked long hours to earn enough money to support us. In my adult life, I have plenty of time to spend with my children. I can have an active life beyond my job, and vacation, travel, and shopping are also available to me. I am confident that when I drive to the grocery store, my car will not break down, and I will get back home without incident. When I was young, our car was old and used and it was not unusual for it to break down. I am confident that every month my bills will get paid; I do not need to juggle payments month to month. These are luxuries my mom never knew. As a college professor, I share information with people who may have never understood mathematics. As chair of the department, I can also ensure that positive changes are made in a system that is there to serve students.

What do I do to replenish my energy? Where do I find joy and comfort? I love sports and music. I am game for a round of chess, golf, or tennis—you name it. I enjoy dancing to Latin or Motown music, and I like listening to jazz, Latin, and Motown tunes. A good book is always appealing, as are good friends. Experiencing a different part of the world with my adorable son or doing anything he likes is my number one joy.

The most important advice I can give is to listen to your inner spirit with the confidence, belief, faith, and knowledge that you have the ability to achieve your goals. I don't believe we are ever given a dream without also being given the ability to achieve that dream. I now know we Latinos are sturdy and can survive anywhere—*somos como nopales*.

Part II
Al Norte

CHAPTER 4

Our History, My Life

Elizabeth Rodríguez-Johnson
Senior Policy Analyst

My story emphasizes a historical perspective on the contributions Mexican Americans have made, for almost five hundred years, to the development of what we know as the United States of America. I choose to place my own story within this historical context because I believe that to understand my career development, it is important to understand the historical and political circumstances that have had a significant impact on my development as a person and as a scientist. As Edén Torres explains in her book *Chicana without Apology*, the historical events of our community reverberate in our individual lives, and it is no less so for me, a daughter of a working-class family from a strip of land called the border, which was the contested space that caused the war between Mexico and the United States in the middle of the nineteenth century (Torres 2003).

Although Latinos are a prominent group in America, few of their contributions to American society are mentioned in history texts. The nineteenth-century American poet Walt Whitman, living at the time of the Mexican-American War, wrote, "I have an idea that there is much of importance about the Latin race contributions to American nationality in the South and Southwest that will never be put with sympathetic understanding and tact on the record" (Whitman 1887). It was clear to him that historians would not recognize Latino participation in the development of the United States. Indeed, his prediction of such an omission has proven true.

A noted Chicano scholar offers an explanation for this woeful omission. According to Gary Archuleta (see Parrillo 1985), during the Mexican-American War and the Spanish-American War, propaganda was used to turn sentiment against the enemy. Latinos were characterized notoriously as criminals or bandidos and as lazy and stupid. A negative public image of Mexicans was needed to justify the wars. The propaganda campaign was effective, and to this day continues to have a lingering effect on the public image of Mexicans and the descendants of those who fought in the wars, as well as all those who have come to this country since.

Early Years

I was born and raised in San Benito, Texas, a small town in the lower Rio Grande Valley, in the very area contested and fought over during the Mexican-American War, which ended in 1848 with the signing of the Treaty of Guadalupe Hidalgo. The daughter and granddaughter of Tejanos, I grew up speaking Spanish as a first language. San Benito is close to the Mexican border town of Matamoros, and my neighborhood extended to the northern Mexican state of Tamaulipas. As cultural geographer Daniel Arreola claims, this area is certainly a cultural region where the geopolitical border is an inconvenience (Arreola 2002). Mine was a totally Mexican American neighborhood.

I was the fourth in a family of eight children. To say we were of meager means is an understatement. Although my family did not participate in welfare, as others did in my community, I did grow up in subsidized housing. This part of the lower Rio Grande Valley has always had a per capita income well below the national average, and we were among some of the poorest living on the poor side of town. As a child, my socioeconomic status did not have a significant impact on me because I attended a Mexican American segregated elementary school. But San Benito had only one junior high, and that is where the glaring differences in economic status between the haves and have-nots first became apparent to me.

I always knew that getting an education was a necessary goal in achieving a better life. Because I was embarrassed of my socioeconomic status, I aspired to do well in school. I remember, as a child, watching Audrey Hepburn in the movie *Sabrina*, in which a girl from a lower socioeconomic position marries into a rich family. My mother impressed upon me that those types of stories were true only in the movies. She told me I would have to buy my own ticket out of my neighborhood—no one would buy it for me. I remember feeling I was alone. That was my first realization that no one would come to my rescue, and that, as the Mariah Carey song "Hero" puts it, "the hero lies in me." It took me many years to realize that my life would not be one of sitting back and enjoying the ride, but rather one of fighting my own fights.

Language Matters

Like many others growing up along the border during the 1950s and 1960s, I understood some English—both my parents spoke it—but I lived in a predominantly Spanish-speaking neighborhood and, as a result, all my communication was in Spanish. I spoke no English when

I entered the first grade. The elementary school I attended was entirely Mexican American. Speaking Spanish on the school grounds was not allowed, regardless of whether you could speak English. If you were caught speaking Spanish, you were punished. I was paddled several times because someone told the teacher I was using Spanish during recess. I was nearly held back in the first grade because of my poor English skills. Although I was not held back, many of my classmates were. I found this sad and unfair, because my classmates were then categorized as less intelligent.

Some of my earliest childhood recollections are my struggles with the English language. I did not particularly like the language because I did not feel comfortable speaking it. I found it difficult to communicate my thoughts and feelings, no matter how hard I tried. While I cannot say so with certainty, I believe this is why I became more interested in mathematics. Solving math problems does not require a mastery of the English language. Therefore, at a very early age I devoted much more time and energy to mastering mathematics rather than English.

This extra effort resulted in my receiving better grades in mathematics, which fed my motivation to do as well as I could in the subject. My accomplishments also became a source for getting attention. As a middle child, I did everything I could to be noticed. In my eyes, the older siblings were special by virtue of their birth order. Similarly, the younger ones were special because they were younger. There seemed to be nothing special about a middle child. I had to work to make myself special. Mathematics became a vehicle for getting the attention I craved.

Con Ganas, o No Ganas—No Guts, No Glory

I realized I could not excel in English, so I focused on math. I remember my third-grade teacher saying to me, "My goodness, Elizabeth" (she was one of the few people who called me Elizabeth), "if you continue to do this well in math, you will surely be successful some-day." I asked my older sister what *successful* meant, because I knew it was something positive. So, at an early age, I associated doing well in math as a positive objective. The better I did in math, the more recognition I received for working hard. The harder I worked, the more proficient I became. The reinforcement I received for being well above average served to fuel my motivation, so I continued to work hard. The effort was well worth it, because it helped me establish a sense of self-worth. Thus, math became a tool for battling my low self-esteem.

Despite achieving academic success and economic security, low self-esteem plagued me for many years to come. When you grow up with a certain mind-set, it takes time to overcome the negative side effects. I became keenly aware of this as a result of my attempts to help others overcome their fear of mathematics.

I believe everyone has an aptitude for math, but many are discouraged by their early experiences. In my opinion, the average person loses interest in math, this worsens with time, and an almost insurmountable psychological barrier against all things mathematical develops. I was fortunate that my early experiences with math were positive, but this is probably not true of the average person. For instance, while a math instructor at a community college, I encountered a young lady whose fear of math was mostly psychological. After the first class, she told me she would fail my class and was only telling me to minimize the embarrassment she would face when she did. I told her I had a secret way of predicting who would and would not fail my classes, and that she was definitely on the not-fail list. I told her I would help her as much as I could, but that she had to work to make my prediction come true. She worked extremely hard throughout the class and passed with a B. One semester later, she told me she had taken the second algebra class and passed that with a B as well. This case confirmed my suspicions that our biggest barrier to achievement can be our perception of our ability to succeed.

Discovering Our History

While I was growing up, I suffered from very low self-esteem. I believe low self-esteem is one of the biggest barriers Mexican American women and girls have to face. It is a phenomenon characteristic of many children who grow up in a lower socioeconomic class. For Chicanas, improving our self-esteem becomes just as important as building our professional skills.

My insecurities stemmed from numerous factors, but I am certain that our socioeconomic status and the stigma of Mexican Americans as inherently ignorant were two of those factors. I clearly remember my seventh-grade history teacher describing the cowardly Mexicans who slaughtered the brave Americans at the Alamo. From this lesson, I concluded that Mexican Americans were not only ignorant but cowardly, too. It was not until my freshman year in college that a history professor said the Mexicans had every right to take the Alamo because it was their property. They had warned the Americans to leave, or lose their lives. Furthermore, the professor noted that numerous Americans at the Alamo, including Colonel Travis and Davy Crockett, were mercenaries.

I have heard it said that history is to a nation what memory is to a people. If this profound statement is true, and I believe it is, then a negative image of your ancestry can have a significant impact on your self-worth. In my case, negative stereotypes only added to my low self-esteem.

The erasure of our positive role in history and the emphasis on negative stereotypes of Latinos in this country gravely affected me. However, Latinos have long played a prominent role in the American experience. To begin with, no other group, except Native Americans, can claim longer residence in America. The first European conquerors, explorers, colonizers, and settlers were our ancestors. On April 11, 1512, Juan Ponce de León landed on the coast of what became the state of Florida. Almost a century before the first English colonists arrived, in 1526, Lucas Vázquez de Ayllón led an expedition of Spaniards to the spot near Jamestown. Hernando de Soto, who began his exploration of North America in 1539, is credited with exploring the lands that today are the states of Alabama, Georgia, the Carolinas, Tennessee, Louisiana, and Arkansas. In 1541, de Soto arrived at the mouth of the Mississippi. But none of my American history books in school mentioned these early explorers of lands that ultimately became the United States of America.

Spanish explorers reached San Francisco, California, in 1542, and Oregon in 1543. Francisco Vásquez de Coronado, in 1540, led an expedition of Spanish soldiers and Indian allies into the area that later became Arizona and New Mexico. He also traveled into what is now Texas and Kansas. On April 30, 1598, Don Juan de Oñate arrived from Mexico at an area near present-day El Paso, Texas, and celebrated the first documented "Thanksgiving." Oñate proclaimed sovereignty over the land for the king of Spain. A noted historian, Sheldon Hall, cited this proclamation as one of the greatest historical events in U.S. history, comparable to the landing of the Pilgrims at Plymouth, Massachusetts, which was not to occur for more than twenty years (see Brown 2001). Yet Oñate's proclamation is not even mentioned in most history textbooks.

Both before and after Oñate's expedition, Spaniards discovered and explored for Spain two-thirds of what is today the United States, decades before the Pilgrims arrived at Plymouth. Between 1492 and 1603, the Spaniards made the first documented European "discovery" of America, and explored both coasts of North America. They explored the Pacific coastline from Baja California to Alaska, and the Atlantic coastline from the Gulf of Mexico to Labrador.

While the early British and Dutch colonists were still struggling to adapt to the New World, Spanish cities were flourishing throughout southern and western parts of the United States. Saint Augustine, Florida, founded in 1565, was the first permanent Spanish settlement in the continental United States. Santa Fe, New Mexico, founded in 1610, has the distinction of being the oldest capital of any state in the country. When I at last learned these historical facts, I became aware of the disservice my education had done by not instilling in me a sense of history as a Mexican American in the United States.

I also found that the "official history" had ignored the many ways that Latinos have contributed to the country's founding. Latinos have historically been quick in responding to the defense of the United States. They were instrumental in helping the United States win its independence from British control. King Juan Carlos of Spain granted a credit of one million pounds to the early American colonists to fight the British. As the financial condition of the Continental (American) army worsened, funds were furnished by Cuba to continue the struggle for freedom. The women of Cuba contributed their jewelry, thereby providing pivotal help to finance the Battle of Yorktown, which numerous historians have labeled as the decisive battle of the Revolutionary War.

My history includes the fact that, for better or worse, and for more than three centuries, the Spanish Crown encouraged the settlement of the American Southwest through the establishment of many religious missions. Franciscan friars were the missionaries who founded most of the missions in Texas, New Mexico, California, and Arizona. Although I was disturbed to learn how some missions carried out their project of

Christianizing the native people, who were also my ancestors, I cannot deny that this missionary past gives me a sense of ownership, which also lends me a sense of place and identity.

In the very land where I grew up, the Texas ranching economy can be traced back to the establishment of these Spanish missions. Every expedition that founded a mission brought along farm animals and experienced hands. In San Antonio, for example, every mission had its own ranch, where cattle products, such as meat, leather, hoof, and horn, became the economic base of the missions. Franciscan and Jesuit missionaries traveled from Zacatecas and Guanajuato into what was then the northern frontier of New Spain to establish settlements in the Southwest. Franciscan Friar Junipero Serra was instrumental in the construction of a large number of California missions. Serra, Father Kino in Arizona, and Father Massanet in Texas are often considered the main architects behind the success of the Spanish missions in the Southwest. This is also my national history.

Nicolás Kanellos has written about the vital role that the mission movement had in California, where Latino mestizo settlers from Mexico intermarried with indigenous populations and the Franciscans not only founded townships and villages but also established a prosperous agricultural and ranching industry (see, for example, Kanellos 1993). Father Serra, Father Kino, and other missionaries founded the missions at San Francisco, Santa Clara, San Diego, Santa Cruz, Nuestra Señora de Los Angeles, Santa Inez, and Santa Barbara in California, and the missions at Espada, San José, Concepcion, San Fernando, and what is today known as the Alamo in San Antonio, Texas.

Another interesting and important contribution from Spanish culture is the right of community property, a law that has greatly aided the rights of women. Based on Spanish-Mexican law, this legacy of the Southwest acknowledges the economic contributions of a wife during marriage, and has been called one of the most important landmarks of Spanish civilization in America.

Latinos have made other significant contributions to American culture that are too numerous to mention, but one in particular is significant to me and my upbringing in Texas, where the ranching tradition was everywhere and all important. The era of the cowboy is one of the most colorful periods of American history. However, it is rarely mentioned that the Spanish brought the horses to the New World. Much of the language associated with the Spanish ranching tradition made its way into the English vernacular of the cowboy. Words for almost every item used by the cowboy, including utensils, methods, and equipment, were adapted from the Mexican vaquero's Spanish. Some of the many examples include *rodeo*, *lasso*, *chaps*, *stirrup tips*, *rope halter*, *ten-gallon hat*, and terms describing roping and horse-breaking techniques. The word *lariat*, for example, comes from *la riata*. Even the system of branding and registering cattle is of Mexican origin. Despite my proximity to the ranching tradition, this rich history was not available to me as I was developing my identity and sense of self-worth.

If I had had some knowledge of my people's history growing up, I am convinced that my low self-esteem would not have been a problem. Rejection of my language and culture by the dominant group as I perceived it in the schools of Texas had a tremendous impact on my psyche. Luckily, I had a loving family as well as mentors in the form of teachers who believed in me, so I was able to survive and succeed.

Career

When I was fourteen, my family moved to Las Cruces, New Mexico. My mother's family lived in that area, and we hoped my father could find more stable employment there. I attended and graduated from

Las Cruces High School and went on to New Mexico State University, where I earned a BS in secondary education, majoring in mathematics. I continued my studies, earning a master's and PhD in educational management and development, with a minor in experimental statistics.

When I graduated, I was recruited by the manager of the mathematics branch at the Pacific Missile Test Center (PMTC) in Point Mugu, California. Because I had degrees in both mathematics and statistics, I was an ideal candidate for the type of work done at this branch. I worked at PMTC for four years, developing mathematical models for missile tracking, and I also provided mathematical formulations of other physical and engineering problems.

For example, my responsibility in the Trident Missile Program was to conduct an analysis of data provided by a survey of deep ocean transponders implanted in the Pacific Ocean. This type of analysis was conducted to help locate the missile. My particular analysis provided distances between the transponders and their depths, in order to determine ocean bottom reference points. Another example of my work was in support of PMTC's participation in the navy's High Energy Laser program. In particular, I was responsible for developing the experimental design of target response tests. I also performed statistical analyses of the resultant target vulnerability data to determine kill modes of generic target subsystems. This study provided a guide for optimizing future directed energy target vulnerability testing.

After being at PMTC for four years, I was accepted into the Office of Personnel Management Women's Executive Leadership Program, which was designed to give women the opportunity to receive management training. I moved to the Washington DC area and began my first assignment, working with the House of Representatives side of the Committee on Science and Technology Policy. I also worked with the Office of Management and Budget (OMB). Because of the high-energy laser work I had done at PMTC, I eventually landed with the Strategic Defense Initiative Organization (SDIO) program, more commonly known as President Reagan's Star Wars program. I stayed with SDIO three years, working in several different positions, first with the Directed Energy Office and later with the Sensors Office.

I left SDIO to take a promotion with the Office of the Director of Operational Test and Evaluation (ODOT&E), where I provided technical expertise and compliance support to ensure that Department of Defense (DoD) major defense weapon systems conformed to operational testing policies and procedures. I examined test policies and procedures as they applied to each system from all perspectives relating to RAM/suitability. Other responsibilities included assisting the ODOT&E staff as required in reviewing operational test plans for adequacy, and evaluating the results of operational testing to determine the suitability of the system tested. My work at ODOT&E took me to many locations, including Sydney, Australia, where I was a part of the U.S. operational test team participating in U.S.–Australian amphibious assault exercises.

After ODOT&E, I worked with the Office of the Director of Defense Research and Engineering (ODDR&E). The most interesting aspect of my tenure at ODDR&E was my two-year assignment to the White House Office of Science and Technology Policy (OSTP), headed by the president's science advisor. I was a senior policy analyst within the OSTP science division. In this position, I coordinated science and engineering activities across federal agencies by surfacing and resolving science and engineering issues with respect to those activities. For example, I assisted with the formulation of two new committees within the newly created National Science and Technology Council (NSTC). I provided coordination among their activities to ensure consistency with the direction provided by the president's science advisor through the Committee on Fundamental Science and the Committee on Health, Safety, and Food Research and Development. This required that I maintain close coordination with cognizant staff in the OMB, the National Science Foundation, NASA, the DoD, the Department of Agriculture, the Department of Health and Human Services, and other federal agencies with large science programs. I exercised crosscutting responsibilities such as budget, legislation, or private sector interaction on NSTC program initiatives.

After my two-year detail at the White House, I went back to the Pentagon and ODDR&E. Because of my background in testing, I went to work for the Office of the Director, Test, Systems Engineering and Evaluation. I was the director of the Y2K management office, working directly for the Principal Deputy Under Secretary of Defense (PDUSD) Acquisition, Technology and Logistics (AT&L). I supported the DoD effort to ensure proper operation of military systems after the millennium rollover.

The Y2K problem resulted from the use of only two digits to represent the year (for example, "98" instead of "1998") when lines of computer codes were designed. At the new millennium (year 2000), the year designated as "00" could have been interpreted by computer systems as "1900," which could have caused huge problems for systems that subtracted dates to calculate elapsed time, and might have caused systems to simply cease functioning when their computers did not recognize the correct date. Because the DoD had such a large number of systems potentially affected by the Y2K problem, the systems were divided into separate functional areas for tracking. I had oversight responsibility for seven functional areas: logistics, weapons systems, procurement, environmental security, science and engineering, facilities and installations, and nuclear, chemical, and biological. My responsibilities entailed assisting the seven corresponding AT&L princi-pal staff assistants with planning their activities, monitoring execution of these activities, transmitting direction to them from PDUSD (AT&L), and providing guidance to the military services to fully understand the status of systems, interfaces, and testing.

My civil service career has offered me many opportunities, one of them being the opportunity to see the world. My job has taken me from Europe and the Scandinavian countries to Australia, and certainly through most of the United States.

Life's Lessons

While I do not believe society owes me anything by virtue of my ethnicity or gender, I do believe there is a bias in this country against the Mexican American. I believe that if all things were equal, then things would be equal. But they are not. I have learned that we cannot rely on others to change the system. We must do it ourselves, lest we become victims of the worst injustice of all, self-pity.

From my many experiences in business, I have learned that one of the biggest losers in this imbalance is the American public. As long as there is a segment of the population that is underutilized, the American public loses the benefits that the untapped talent could produce.

I believe that as Americans first, Mexican Americans owe this coun-try the devotion necessary to change and improve it. When we use our talents and support others like us to do the same, we make the United States an even stronger nation. Also, we provide this country with the type of energy that will continue to make us one of the most powerful nations in the world.

Works Cited

Arreola, Daniel. 2002. *Tejano South Texas: A Mexican American Cultural Province.* Austin: University of Texas Press.

Brown, Michelle J. 2001. "Historical Revisionists Work to Set Historical Record Straight." *West Texas County Courier,* p. 1.

Kanellos, Nicolás, ed. 1993. *Reference Library of Hispanic America.* 3 vols. Detroit: Gale.

Parrillo, Vincent. 1985. *Strangers to These Shores: Race and Ethnic Relations in the United States.* New York: John Wiley and Sons.

Torres, Edén E. 2003. *Chicana without Apology: The New Chicana Cultural Studies.* Oxford: Routledge.

Whitman, Walt. 1887. "Walt Whitman Gossips of His Sojourn Here Years Ago as a Newspaper Writer. Notes of His Trip Up the Mississippi and to New York." *New Orleans Picayune,* January 25.

CHAPTER 5

¡Claro Que Sí Se Puede!

Lupita D. Montoya
Assistant Professor of Environmental Engineering

Our deepest fear is not that we are inadequate. Our deepest fear is that we are powerful beyond measure. It is our light, not our darkness, that most frightens us. We ask ourselves, who am I to be brilliant, gorgeous, talented, and fabulous? Actually, who are you not to be? You are a child of God. Your playing small doesn't serve the world. There's nothing enlightened about shrinking so that other people won't feel insecure around you. We are all meant to shine, as children do. We are born to make manifest the glory of God that is within us. It's not just in some of us, it's in everyone. And as we let our own light shine, we unconsciously give other people permission to do the same. As we are liberated from our own fear, our presence automatically liberates others.

–Marianne Williamson, *A Return to Love: Reflections on the Principles of A Course in Miracles* (mistakenly attributed to Nelson Mandela and his 1994 inauguration speech)

I was born in Culiacán, the capital of the state of Sinaloa, in the northwest corner of Mexico. My mother was only seventeen when I was born. Two years after my birth, she was divorced and expecting a second child. After the divorce, my father disappeared from our lives and we moved in with my grandparents. By the time I was five, my mother had moved to the United States and left us with my grandparents. By then, there were three of us, the youngest only nine months old when my mother left. My mother moved to Los Angeles, California, and worked in the garment district for many years. Like many other unfortunate Mexican families, she sacrificed to feed and clothe her children. Amazingly enough, my grandmother had lived a very similar story when she left her small town for Culiacán, leaving two small children with her parents. It took me a very long time to realize how painful it must have been to be away from their children. Now I recognize it was the best they could offer their families under the circumstances. In spite of all these sad events, I remember my childhood as a very happy one and truly believe I was lucky to have lived with my grandparents. I especially loved my grandmother, Lupita Cuén de Garfio, who was an extraordinary human being and whom I considered my real mother for as long as I can remember. These early experiences have had a tremendous impact on the way I live my life and make decisions to this day. Above all, I decided I did not want to subject myself or my children to a life without the stability and love that a healthy family enjoys. During numerous occasions while growing up, I distinctly remember saying, "This will not happen to my children."

Being the oldest child automatically put me in a position of responsibility. I was expected to set the example for my siblings, and for the most part I accepted the challenge. My grandmother had a very effective way of disciplining me. She would simply say, "Indachacha, *esas cosas no se hacen*" (Indachacha, those things are simply not done). Indachacha was my nickname, which came from *linda muchacha* (pretty girl). I cherished that nickname because it always made me feel pretty and loved. Her light but firm reprimands would be enough to make me think twice about whatever I was doing. I must admit that many times I would not necessarily agree with her, but I would take the time to reason things out so that I could defend my choices. I believe that her quiet way of reprimanding me trained me to think carefully about my actions, and taught me to plan and take my future seriously.

As a child, I was always at the top of my class and involved in school activities. I enjoyed being smart and having lots of friends. I also liked making my grandparents proud of me. My grandfather,

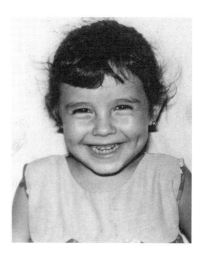

Lupita D. Montoya, circa 1968.

Isidro Garfio, told stories about how my grandmother loved to go to the schools' open houses and meetings because the teachers always said nice things about me and the quality of my work. The joke was that she would send my grandpa to the meetings with my brother's teachers, because they would usually relay some embarrassing comments on his less-than-stellar performance. My younger sister, Lourdes, was also a very good student, and often had the difficult task of redeeming our family's name after my brother's performance.

One early experience that has had a long-lasting impact on my life occurred when I was in third or fourth grade. I remember walking to school with several of my classmates. As we walked, we discussed the homework that was due that day. As expected, we compared notes, and as it turned out, everyone had done the homework the same way except me. After some discussion, I was persuaded to conform to the group and change my answer. I kept thinking about the homework without any further discussion with my friends. By the time we got to school, I had decided that I was initially right, so I changed my answer back to my original solution. As it turned out, I was the only one who got the right answer that day. After that experience, I had a healthy confidence in my own abilities and have tried to hold on to that confidence through my entire academic career. This and other experiences were extremely helpful whenever I faced people who tried to convince me that I was not smart enough or that my accomplishments were the results of affirmative action. Having self-confidence can make or break an academic career, so I am very fortunate to have developed that aspect of my personality before I came to this country, where people often judge you before knowing you or your abilities. I must admit that I have faced self-doubt on many occasions, but I have always emerged more confident than before. The issue is that each new challenge is bigger than or different from the previous one. The good news is that all these challenges enrich your life, and before you know it, you have the life that you always dreamed of.

Ever since I was a child, I absolutely loved school. I dreaded summer vacations, because I would not go to classes or see my friends for a couple of months. Even though we would usually travel to Los Angeles to visit my mother, I would often prefer to stay home and continue my happy routine. Elementary school and junior high school were rather uneventful, but filled with good friends and academic achievement. By the end of junior high, I had discovered boys, but had an unusual reaction to them. On the one hand, I enjoyed the attention I received, but I could not bear the idea of having someone dictate my whereabouts or actions (as was often the case with the other girls.) To this day, my first boyfriend still reminds me of how long I refused to date him on the grounds that I did not want him to get any ideas of owning me. Interestingly, he eventually convinced me, and we dated for some time and have remained friends for over twenty-five years. He still calls me every year from Mexico to wish me a happy birthday, and I look forward to his calls. I am convinced that I was reluctant to become subservient to someone (as a partner, for example) because I saw such relationships enough times to determine that I would not let it happen to me, whatever the cost. In that light, I was ready to spend my life on my own, if necessary.

The Start of a New Life

By the time I was sixteen, my mother had remarried, become a U.S. citizen, and arranged for us to immigrate. I was the first of her three children to move to Los Angeles to live with her. I initially thought I would only stay in the city for a year, long enough to learn English, and go back to Mexico to start college there. As it turned out, when I got to LA, I was sent to high school due to my age and my lack of English proficiency or a high school diploma. I enrolled in Grant High School, in Van Nuys, California, as a junior once my courses from Mexico had been evaluated and properly transferred. I became one of thousands of ESL (English as a Second Language) students in the Los Angeles Unified School District. I managed to learn English within a few months by judiciously avoiding sitting next to Spanish-speaking students and by cultivating friendships with people of other ethnicities. Besides learning a new language, I wanted to stay at the top of my class, as I was used to. That was a bit hard at first, but soon I recovered my footing. Two years later, I graduated as the first Hispanic valedictorian in the history of my high school. My name should still be posted there for the year 1983. While at Grant High School, I had wonderful teachers (Mrs. Krupa, Mrs. Feldman, Mrs. Winningham, Mrs. Palley, Mrs. Diamond, and Mrs. Golditch), who took the time to advise me and make sure I stayed on a good track; they even changed my schedule once to place me with a better teacher.

I have great memories of my high school years at Grant, and hope that one day I can repay some of the goodwill I received there.

Interestingly, my sister Lourdes, who was previously a science teacher there, now holds the position of ESL coordinator. She is doing a great job, but often tells me of the challenges she faces dealing with students who cannot get up to speed quickly enough or who get into trouble before they can secure their move to college. The saddest stories, however, are those about kids who succumb to stressful family situations or negative influences and will never fulfill their potential. My hope is that this book will help young students, who may doubt their abilities, to overcome their challenges. My message to them is that no matter what life throws at you, you have the last word. You choose whether you push forward or settle for what was given to you.

By my senior year at Grant, I had decided to go to college in the United States. In spite of my good grades, my mother insisted I attend California State University, Northridge (CSUN), so that I could live at home and take the bus to school. We reached the agreement that I would go to CSUN for two years and then transfer to the University of California, Los Angeles, my preferred school. I enrolled at CSUN, ultimately never transferred out, and, as in high school, loved my experiences there. I started as a chemistry major because I wanted to work "making drugs" in an area now known as pharmaceuticals. During my first semester at Northridge, I was contacted by the university's Minority Engineering Program (MEP) counselor, Milton Randall, who had my entrance proficiency exam scores for science and math in hand. Because engineering was an impacted major (that is, more students applied than could be accepted), MEP wanted to recruit only minority students who had solid math and science backgrounds. As Milton explained the advantages of a degree in engineering versus chemistry, I remembered that I had indeed planned to become a chemical engineer when I was in Mexico. That early decision was based on a positive experience I had with a teacher who was an engineer and whom I admired very much. Because I also enjoyed and excelled in math, it made sense to me to return to my original plan, so I officially changed my major to engineering after just a few weeks in college. I have never regretted that decision.

My years as an undergraduate engineering student were marked by several ups and downs. First, I found that my English skills were still too poor to completely keep up my grades. Again, I worked extra hard to achieve the level of proficiency I needed to excel. After each class, I often had a list of words I did not know and had to look up to make sense of my lectures. Another major obstacle I faced was my often problematic and unsupportive family life. I found my engineering studies to be very demanding, and having to complete all of my schoolwork by myself at home in the midst of continuous noise and family turmoil proved to be very difficult. A constant problem involved a couple of my siblings, who for one reason or another seemed always to be in trouble. Also, I was not allowed to stay at school past my class time to work with other students on my homework. It took a couple of years for my mother to accept that something needed to change. I think her change of heart occurred when she heard from other parents how they supported their children, and the sacrifices it took for them to graduate. After this change, college life started to improve for me. I worked part-time, bought my own car, and paid my own way through school with minimal help from home. Later, I moved out of the house, and once again I was able to excel academically. My early college experience has given me an appreciation for people who, despite difficult circumstances, do not give up and eventually prevail. I am also a strong believer in giving children a safe and quiet place to study.

Surviving Engineering

As much as I enjoyed my time at CSUN, I was ready to graduate and move on. While I was there, I was involved in student activities, including student government, because I really enjoyed working with people, and it provided a good balance to my intellectual pursuits. By my last year at CSUN, I was completely self-supporting, doing very well academically, and eager to continue learning. Based on my affinity for subjects such as fluid mechanics and thermodynamics, and my interest in emissions control from cars, I had decided to pursue graduate studies in the area of air pollution control from internal combustion engines. I had also developed into an outspoken advocate for the rights of minorities and females to pursue engineering, which often got me into "interesting" discussions. Positioned between peers who claimed that unqualified minorities were taking summer jobs from other "qualified" (meaning white) students, and my own people, who wanted me to settle for lower standards of achievement and aspiration, I was simply ready for the next stage in my life.

Somehow I had the presence of mind to apply to top graduate programs in mechanical engineering. I applied to several schools, keeping in mind their rankings and their locations (I have never been a fan of cold weather, so I stuck to universities in California and Texas). I was fortunate to be accepted to the top two programs in mechanical engineering, which also happened to be my top two choices: Stanford University and the University of California, Berkeley. I decided on Stanford because I loved the campus, because it appeared to offer a program in air pollution from combustion processes (my desired area of study), and because it was not as "political" as Berkeley. Knowing my affinity for student activism, I was afraid I might be swept up by the Berkeley culture and lose sight of my academic goals. In retrospect, it was probably a silly concern, but I knew my weaknesses and tried to minimize their negative effect as much as possible. At that time, it seemed wise for me to be in a less controversial, less political environment. Again, I have never regretted this decision, although I am now convinced that my fears about Berkeley were unfounded.

My first quarter at Stanford was extremely hard, to say the least. Once again, I was academically behind most students, who all seemed to come from top universities and from academic families. All I can remember from that initial period is the grayness of the days, the endless homework, and the Loma Prieta earthquake. Because I had been through some earthquakes in LA before, the quake was the least of my worries. I was more preoccupied with making it through the program; in spite of all the work I was putting in, I was still not doing well in some of my classes. On top of that, I discovered the courses I had based my Stanford decision on did not include the type of material I was interested in—air pollution control. Luckily, my advisor at the time, Professor Godfrey Mungal, made me aware of courses in air pollution taught by a new professor in the environmental engineering department. I decided to take those courses and found my passion. Even though I had never taken an environmental engineering course before, I decided I would complete my MS in mechanical engineering with a subspecialty in air pollution, and then apply to the PhD program in environmental engineering. Of course, I also had to convince Professor Lynn Hildemann, the only air pollution expert on campus, that I deserved a chance to join her research group. I remember checking in with her regularly and taking the courses she suggested in order to prove I could do the work. I still remember vividly my conversation with her after taking those courses. I went on and on about how difficult one of the courses had been and how badly I felt about not doing well. She finally stopped me and reminded me that I had A's in my other classes and that I needed to be easier on myself. I appreciated her comments, and especially her willingness to give me the opportunity to prove myself. As it turned out, she did accept me into the program, and I started doing air pollution research in my new department.

Finding Myself Again

After my rough start at Stanford, life settled down again, and I found my place among people who were not threatened by my personality or ambitions. My times in the environmental engineering department at Stanford were among the best of my higher education years. I made great friends, grew both personally and professionally, and even met my future husband. On the other hand, it was also during this period that my grandmother died, which left me in a state of depression for some time. After I had planned my entire life to take care of her during her later years, I was robbed of that opportunity. There was even a period during which I thought I had lost my motivation for continuing my education. Luckily, at about the same time, I met the person who is now my husband. He made a huge difference in my life during this period. He helped me regain my confidence and focus. I am convinced that my grandmother's passing had something to do with my meeting him. Somehow I was compensated for my great loss, and I am still very grateful for this gift.

Completing the PhD program was difficult, but for different reasons than I had initially expected. In fact, I found the hardest part was to push forward even when things did not go well. In my case, my biggest problems generated from home, in the form of new troubles and diseases afflicting my closest family members. I had nightmares and often felt tremendously guilty for not being at home to help out. In fact, the closest I ever came to leaving graduate school was during my grandmother's brief recovery period after her stroke. I was ready to leave school and care for her during her recovery, whether by personally providing all the attention she needed or by working to pay someone who would. As it turned out, I never made the choice to leave school, since she died a few days after the slight recovery from her stroke.

People and Events

Throughout my life, I consciously looked at both good and bad examples, and made choices based on what I learned. Ever since I was a child, I knew I wanted to be educated, be married to someone who treated me as an equal or not married at all, and have a career helping people. I was particularly reluctant to become someone's less-than-equal partner. That eliminated a lot of options for me, but I was not worried one bit. Growing up without a father left me with a healthy skepticism toward male figures. Fortunately, I have met wonderful men who have mentored and helped me along the way, so my opinion of the male species has changed a great deal.

While at CSUN, I often talked to the director of the MEP, Rick Ainsworth, who is now working in that same capacity at UCLA. Rick is an energetic and optimistic person, a real go-getter, always trying to encourage students to excel. I remember talking to him about graduate school and studying policy so that I could help "my people." At that time, I had started to consider a PhD in education, thinking that would be a good way to reach my goals. He asked me if I liked engineering, and I said I not only liked it, I really loved it. He then suggested I stick with it and get a PhD in engineering. "That degree will give you more credibility than many other degrees," he said. It made sense to me, so I stuck with engineering. I know of other students who, in that same situation, were steered away from their chosen field in science or engineering, so in that respect, I was lucky. Rick gave me a good piece of advice and showed confidence in my abilities. To this day, I consider him one of the most influential people in my early career.

Another very important person in my professional life has been Dr. Noé Lozano, the associate dean of minority student affairs in the School of Engineering at Stanford. Dr. Lozano comes closest to the father figure I envisioned I should have had but missed out on. While I believe there is nothing wrong with knowing that you deserved better in life, I do view using the excuse of a missing parent or a bad upbringing for poor choices as wrong. Recognizing the good in other people can help us grow and avoid the vicious cycle of dysfunctional relationships or poor choices.

Dr. Lozano was involved in my recruitment into Stanford, and while I was there, he helped me in many ways. I was one of four Chicanas recruited into engineering the year I began my master's degree. Of those four students, I was the only one who stayed on for a PhD. I know Dr. Lozano would have loved to have us all stay, but unfortunately it did not work out that way. Since I initially came as a student in mechanical engineering, I was disappointed to discover that that department did not offer a program that appealed to me. In addition, I found that department unwelcoming and harsh, not the kind of place where I wanted to spend my next few years. Fortunately, I had the support of Dr. Lozano and received financial support for a couple of quarters while I transferred to the environmental engineering department, where a new program in air pollution was starting up. That assistance proved crucial to my ability to stay at Stanford. It gave me time to prove myself in a new discipline, and to build my confidence so that I could successfully pursue a PhD. Dr. Lozano also provided support at extremely sensitive times, such as when my grandmother died and when my project was not making progress due to lack of funding. Overall, he gave me the most important advice I received while at Stanford. For as long as I live, I will be grateful for his time and efforts.

Although I do not usually talk much about my PhD advisor, she has been absolutely great to me over the years. Dr. Lynn Hildemann was the only female engineering professor I had in my entire higher education career. Since I went to Stanford with a clear vision of wanting to do air pollution research, running into her was truly fortuitous. Unlike me, Dr. Hildemann had a father who was also a college professor. In fact, many of my peers at Stanford came from academic families as well. It seemed as if some of them had no other choice but to pursue a PhD. In some cases, it was obvious that the decision was made for them or that their reasons for being in a PhD program were not the right ones. That was certainly not the case with my advisor; she was fully qualified and seemed to truly love her work. She has been an important example for me. Dr. Hildemann came from a top-notch university (the California Institute of Technology), where she was trained among the top scientists in our field. In spite of these "advantages," she still faced numerous obstacles, including family losses and gender bias, along the way. Her example has been inspiring, and even after graduating from her group, I still asked for her advice when making career choices. Thanks to her guidance and support, I graduated as the first Chicana in the history of the environmental engineering program at Stanford. Not surprisingly, there were other "firsts" graduating in other departments at that time and since then.

The most influential person in my life, however, has been my husband, Ken Jansen. Ken has challenged many of my misconceptions and prejudices, and has been a great partner and cheerleader. With him, I have been able to build the life that I dreamed of when I was a child. These words are deceptively direct and simple; it has taken an enormous amount of work for me to reach this point. Based on my personal experience, I wanted to delay marriage until I was absolutely sure it was the right decision. Deciding to have children was even harder, not because of the "burden" they could put on my career, but because of my ever present need to guarantee their right to a stable and complete family. That is clearly a fear left over from growing up without my natural parents. Because Ken was raised in the Midwest by parents of German descent who have been married over sixty years now, our upbringings were quite different. Nevertheless, we share core principles that keep us together and working as a team.

When we met at Stanford, Ken was already finishing his PhD, while I was starting mine. It was obvious to us that there would be a geographic separation at some point as we pursued our academic careers. Although he managed to do a postdoctoral fellowship on campus so that we could stay together longer, eventually he had to leave. He wanted to join a faculty in mechanical engineering at a good research institution. At that time, I was not sure if I wanted to take the same path. I had entered Stanford thinking I would return to CSUN to teach. We worked together on the decision of which offer to accept, but after his interviews, I knew what his preference was. We agreed that Rensselaer Polytechnic Institute (RPI) in Troy, New York, was the best choice, because of its reputation and its great fit for his research. Unfortunately, the school was in upstate New York, entirely across the country. In the summer of 1996, we drove across the country to move Ken, and after a few weeks I returned to Stanford to finish my degree. Unfortunately (but not surprisingly), finishing the degree took longer than we anticipated, and we were separated two extra years. The last year of this separation, we married. As I wrapped up my research, I consulted often with my advisor, Dr. Hildemann, about my plans to leave for New York and write my thesis there. She was always supportive, even during incredibly stressful times. In the summer of

1998, I gathered my data and my belongings and made the move across the country for the second time. By the time I arrived in Troy, we had bought a house and I had a postdoc fellowship lined up for the next year.

Career and Life Choices: *The Latest Challenges*

During my first few months in New York, I wrote, defended, and submitted my thesis, moved into our new house, and started a new academic position at the State University of New York (SUNY), Albany. My experience at my new job was initially positive, but after a few months it became disappointing. My advisor at the time turned out to be the antithesis of what I expected a female scientist to be. I can honestly say that I was at my wit's end after a few months. I had long and difficult conversations with my husband about the stress I was under, and also about how little time we spent together. Since he was going through the tenure system, he would often work sixteen-hour days while I tried to survive in my new environment.

I finally decided to find a new advisor and to change research projects, and I became head of a small project studying indoor air quality and asthma on a Native American reservation in New York. While I enjoyed working on this project, I was not doing enough engineering work to keep me fully engaged. After a year on the project, I was again confronted with the question of what to do next. I was still seeing little of my husband, and my job situation was far from ideal. Although I liked the people at SUNY, the nature of the research was not technical enough to keep me intellectually stimulated. Meanwhile, RPI was undergoing administration changes, so there would be no prospects of a job for me there anytime soon. Again, I started to discuss possible options, including moving back to California, where I thought I would have more job opportunities. Ken would not hear of it, so we compromised, determining that I would find a position within driving distance.

After some research, I found a program in Boston that seemed like a great match. The Harvard School of Public Health (HSPH) had a program in environmental science and engineering that focused on instrumentation development for studies seeking to understand the links between air pollution and health effects. I contacted the professor in charge about a possible postdoctoral position in his lab. After reviewing my qualifications and giving me a personal interview, he asked me to join his group in the early summer of 2000. Ken drove with me to that interview, and we found an apartment nearby so that I could maximize my productivity while there. My work at HSPH was challenging and cutting-edge. My initial project involved testing various sensors for environmental monitoring applications, including what today would be called "homeland security" devices. The downside was that such cutting-edge projects are often risky for postdocs, whose primary goal is to produce publications above all else. As it turned out, the project was ended after a year due to disagreements about intellectual property issues between HSPH and our collaborators, an outside lab.

At this juncture, I found out I was pregnant. I also learned that my initial plan to stay at HSPH for two years could be extended another year, since I had an internal fellowship. I decided to stay at HSPH so that I could work on other projects and produce some publications before leaving. Fortunately, I had a very healthy pregnancy and was able to work up to the day of my delivery. My son was born by caesarean section in January of 2002 at Brigham and Women's Hospital in Boston. His arrival was the best thing I accomplished during my time in that city. After Joshua was born, I took the six weeks of maternity leave that postdocs are entitled to and stretched them to eight weeks by working from my home in New York. I then returned to Boston to finish my projects, and brought my son along. Living with us during this time was a cousin, who stayed with Josh during the day and went to school during the evenings. I had a very tight schedule: working during the day, breast-feeding by pumping at least once a day, and coming home by 5:30 p.m. The schedule and demands were taxing both emotionally and physically, but it was still much better than what followed, when my cousin had to leave and Joshua moved to New York to live with my husband in August of 2002.

After Josh moved to New York, I essentially commuted to Boston. I would drive to Boston for three or four days at a time to complete my laboratory work, and then return to Troy to care for my family and write. A few months of this madness wore me down, and I became over-stressed and depressed. It was simply impossible to maintain my career and family life at a good level. I was physically, emotionally, and intel-lectually exhausted. On top of it all, I felt that I was being blamed for the failure of my first project. I have never been one to shy away from my responsibilities, but I do not take unfair blame well, either. After some time, I concluded there was not much I could do to change the situation, except do my best to complete my projects and move back to Troy to be with my family. As I was finishing my work at HSPH, I worked with a different advisor, who was more supportive and gave me more flexibility to complete my work. By the end of the summer of 2003, I was completely back in Troy, hoping to take a well-deserved vacation to regain my health, get my home back in shape, and enjoy my son.

About this time I heard of a tenure-track faculty opening in the envi-ronmental engineering department at RPI, and I was encouraged to apply. After my interview, I received an offer and started to work within a month. I never took a vacation, but I was ecstatic to be at the same institution as my husband, who was now tenured and doing well. He had had to slow down quite a bit, however, while he was the primary caregiver for Joshua during the previous months. After much discussion, Ken and I again reached an agreement: we made the schedule changes necessary to make sure I was given a fair chance to fight for tenure. Of course, I will never have the luxury to spend sixteen hours a day in the lab, but I do not think I will need it. I intend to make every minute count. What I need most now is to have all my energy and focus in the right places to make sure I make a successful bid for my tenure.

In addition, we intended to have a second child so that Joshua would have a sibling and not be alone when he lost his parents. This may sound morbid to some people, but it is a practical conclusion that two engineers and loving parents can easily reach. As I write this essay, I am happy to say that Isaac is two years old and also a very healthy child. I am now trying to reach yet another, higher level of efficiency so that I can be the mother and the professional I strive to be. This is by far the hardest thing I have ever done, but also the most wonderful. I know a number of people with academic careers who have chosen to have no children or to have only one child. Almost invariably, they have told me, when asked, that they wished they had had one, or more than one, child.

I struggled with the decisions to have a second child and continue my academic career, but I am increasingly convinced that life's successes are not measured by the number of publications, salary, or fame in one's field. For me at least, success is measured by the fulfillment of my childhood dreams: having a stable and loving family, a career that stimulates me intellectually, and a calling that serves my community. To reach these goals takes a lot of effort, but I believe anything worth having in life must be earned through hard work, and I am still up to the challenge.

CHAPTER 6

Mi Viaje en Esta Vida

The Life of a Laredo Girl

Martha Cecilia Zúñiga

Professor of Molecular, Cellular, and Developmental Biology

If we treat people as if they were what they ought to be, then we help them to become what they are capable of being.
—Johann Wolfgang von Goethe, *Wilhelm Meister's Apprenticeship*

Although my father never quoted Goethe, his relationship with his children embodied this quotation. I grew up knowing three things: that whatever I choose to do in life, I must strive to do it to the best of my ability; that my personal integrity is my most important possession; and that my father's love and support would be the beacon of light that would guide me on this wonderful path known as life. Over the years, whenever my confidence has flagged or the obstacles before me have seemed insurmountable, my father's expectations of me and his faith in me have given me the inner strength to carry on. I have always felt that through my performance and deportment, I represent not only myself but also my large family, including my parents, nine siblings, fourteen nephews and nieces, my nephews' three children, my extended family of eighteen uncles and aunts and their spouses, and my ninety first cousins, as well as my hometown of Laredo and my home state of Texas. This is not a burden, but rather a privilege and also a source of comfort, for even when my quest has been lonely, I have never felt completely alone. Wherever I go and whatever I do, I carry my family and the special persona of Laredo in my soul.

> You may have tangible wealth untold:
> Caskets of jewels and coffers of gold.
> Richer than I you can never be—
> I had a Mother who read to me.
>
> —Strickland Gillilan, *The Reading Mother*

My parents have been my guides through life, and they continue to be. However, during my childhood, books were my portals to the world outside of Laredo. My mother, an avid reader herself, read to me as a child and shared with me the joy of reading. When I was very young, she took me to the Laredo public library. One of my proudest moments was the day I was issued my very own library card. When I was old enough to go to the library alone, I would take the city bus downtown on Saturdays and check out as many library books as was permitted, only to read them voraciously in my bed after the family had all gone to sleep. The following Saturday, I would board the bus again and go to the library for a new stack of books. Later, my mother gave me subscriptions to book clubs for birthday presents. In those books, I read about places and lives very different from mine, not necessarily better, but certainly different. As a child, I read novels, and when I exhausted my supply of those, I read the dictionary and Collier's encyclopedia, which my parents kept in the living room. Even now, I love libraries, the smell of books, the feel of their bindings, and the pages between my fingers. I would much rather read a book held in my hands than read text on a computer screen. And for me, an old, well-worn book is preferable to a glossy new one. Once, my brother's girlfriend took my dog-eared copy of John Steinbeck's *East of Eden*. A friend soon replaced it with a new copy, but I did not enjoy it nearly as much, for it did not automatically fall open to the pages bearing my favorite passages.

Although Spanish was the language of my father's childhood, he mastered the English language very well and was eloquent in both tongues. In the evenings, my father worked crossword puzzles in the *Laredo Times* and the *San Antonio Express*, and he invited me to work them with him. It is from him that I learned a love of words. My paternal grandfather was a poet, and from him I acquired the facility for and desire to write verse. Poetry remains my favorite way of expressing my innermost thoughts and feelings.

> The world is so full of a number of things,
> I'm sure we should all be as happy as kings.
> —Robert Louis Stevenson, "Happy Thought," from *A Child's Garden of Verses*

As a child I had many aspirations. I wanted to be a writer; I wanted to sing; I wanted to be a nun and work with the poor people in Latin America; I even wanted to be an artist. I liked to sketch and paint birds, albeit with an untrained hand. At an early age, I also became fascinated by science. A seminal moment came one evening when my father, who had been hunting for rabbits, was cleaning a rabbit that he had killed—not an unusual task, since my *abuelita* loved rabbit and he often hunted them for her. My brother, sisters, and I were out in the backyard playing. While cleaning the rabbit, Daddy discovered it was a pregnant female, and he called me over to see it. There, in the split-open rabbit abdomen, I saw two perfect little baby bunnies, still covered by the translucent amniotic sac. I stared in wonderment at these beautiful baby bunnies.

I was the second of ten children, so by the time this episode occurred, I had seen my mother go through pregnancy several times. I had experienced awe at the kick of a baby's tiny foot beneath my hand placed on her swollen belly, and I had felt a thrill at the sight of the beautiful babies that came home with her from the hospital. The sight of the unborn baby bunnies was mesmerizing. I wanted to understand how an animal developed from a fertilized egg into a perfect little creature, and I wondered why development sometimes occurred flawlessly and why sometimes it went awry. My interest in science probably also was nurtured by the fact that I grew up during an exciting time in science. For example, it was then that the American space program was being developed. To me, science represented a continuum, extending from the exploration of the vast natural world (both known and unknown) to the cells and molecules that dictated the beating of my heart. What could be more exciting?

My parents and grandparents all had a strong belief in the power of knowledge and in the importance of education. For most of my childhood, my mother taught high school math, and early in my childhood my father also was a teacher. However, my early teachers did not encourage me. Indeed,

Martha Cecilia Zúñiga, 1956.

my fourth-grade teacher scornfully referred to me as "the little brown runt." Of course, I felt humiliated by comments such as these. They were among my first evidence of prejudice, which I would encounter again at various stages of my life. I thought then that it would be important to apply myself to doing well, so that people like this teacher would not be able to hold me down.

My meek but dogged persistence paid off. When I was in the eleventh grade in high school, my biology teacher, Federico Reyna, took me aside after class one day and told me about a program sponsored by the National Science Foundation. I was surprised that he had selected me over other students whose confident cockiness in class contrasted with my own shy demeanor. The program to which Mr. Reyna introduced me was called the Summer Science Training Program (SSTP). This program still exists, but under the name Young Scholars Program. Mr. Reyna gave me a brochure to show to my parents. It listed the fifty SSTPs that ran at universities across the United States. My baby brother, the ninth child in the family, was only six months old, and my mother's immediate response to my plea to apply was negative. But my father said I could apply to the program at the University of Texas, Austin, because it was his alma mater, and the program at Loyola University in New Orleans, because it was a Catholic university. I was not accepted at the University of Texas program, but I was accepted at Loyola. I was greatly astonished to be accepted into the Loyola program because the application process included an entrance exam, which was sent to Mr. Reyna and which I took one Saturday morning. This was an exam of trivia, with questions such as "Where is the Taj Mahal?" and "Where is the *Mona Lisa*?" These were questions for which my sheltered life in Laredo had not prepared me, and I was certain that I had failed the exam miserably. But now this did not matter—I was New Orleans bound! My next goal was to attend the program without costing my parents a penny. I had already been earning money babysitting, but now I babysat every weekend so I could save enough money for the airfare from San Antonio to New Orleans. I could barely contain my excitement as I boarded the airplane in San Antonio. I was going to New Orleans, and I had paid for the airline ticket myself!

> If you can meet with triumph and disaster
> And treat those two imposters just the same…
>
> —Rudyard Kipling, "If"

Throughout my primary and secondary school years, I studied diligently. I could study in a house full of boisterous children or in the still quiet of a library. It never occurred to me not to study, not to read. While I earned straight A's, I was not the best student in the class, nor was I as confident as my peers in my high school courses. When I arrived in New Orleans, I was outclassed to an even greater degree by the other SSTP students, at least in terms of preparedness. That summer we SSTP students took college-level lecture and laboratory courses in chemistry, physics, calculus, and computer sciences at Loyola University. Most of the students in the program had already taken physics, calculus, and computer science in high school; I had not. I loved math, so I was particularly chagrined to discover I was woefully unprepared for the calculus class that summer. I also felt appallingly underprepared for the calculus-based physics course. I tried to compensate the only way I knew—by working hard. Frequently, it seemed that all my studying got me no closer to understanding some of the material. In contrast, the coursework seemed so effortless for the other students. They studied minimally and spent many a summer evening on Bourbon Street, while I sat in the university library until it closed. I excelled only in the lab classes, where I was a natural. At the end of the summer, Dr. Christman, director of the program, told me something that has stayed with me ever since. He said that Dr. Vidulic, the educational psychologist who had designed the entrance exam that I had taken in Laredo, predicted that student performance in the program would correlate directly with his or her performance on the trivia test. Dr. Christman was not so sure, and he selected a small number of students who performed poorly on the entrance exam. I was one of this group of students. Dr. Christman told me that I was the outlying data point that defied Dr. Vidulic's prediction. I was both embarrassed and happy at the news. It seemed that hard work would be my ticket to success.

At the end of the program, I was astonished to learn that many of the students who excelled in the coursework nevertheless decided they did not want to major in math or science after all. In contrast, my experiences in the program only strengthened my desire to major in chemistry or biology. The two chemistry lab instructors, Mary Frances and Butch Winkler, as well as one of the student counselors, David Leif Anderson, and Dr. Christman all played important roles in my development at that stage of my education. They advised me, they challenged me, and they supported me. Although this was the first time I had been away from home for more than two weeks, I was not lonely. I developed friendships with SSTP students, students in the Upward Bound Program at Loyola, and people who attended Mass at the Loyola University chapel. I even had a family away from home that summer in New Orleans. Mary Ellen Kuehne, a fellow student, was born and raised in Metairie, a suburb of New Orleans, and a few weekends during that summer, Mary Ellen's family invited me to stay at their house. I felt loved and supported by them. They were a large Catholic family of modest means, and they had a strong work ethic, much like my family in Laredo. Thus, in addition to providing me with intellectual challenges, the summer in New Orleans proved to me that I could find a supportive, nurturing environment away from home.

Just what makes that little old ant
Think he'll move that rubber tree plant
Anyone knows an ant, can't
Move a rubber tree plant.
But he's got high hopes…

—Sammy Cahn and James Van Heusen, "High Hopes"

Perhaps not unexpectedly, my return to Laredo was somewhat of a letdown. I seemed to have nothing in common with my old friends. My mother was pregnant again, for the tenth time, and her pregnancy was not going well. I worried that she might die. I knew in my heart that if my mother died, I would stay in Laredo and help Daddy raise my younger sisters and brothers. I did not discuss these fears with my parents. Perhaps if I had, my worries would have been dispelled; perhaps my imagination was overly vivid. But my mother seemed to be so ill. I worried about her and about my future, even as I applied to colleges and for college scholarships. I will always remember the day that my baby brother was delivered by caesarean section. My senior year of high school was one of the most miserable years of my life, but the day my baby brother was born was one of my happiest. My mother emerged from the delivery happy and well, and I had a new, beautiful baby brother. That summer, I returned to New Orleans as a counselor for Dr. Christman's SSTP at Loyola. I also took courses at the university during both summer terms. The following fall, I enrolled at the University of St. Thomas in Houston on a full scholarship. A year later, I transferred to the University of Texas, Austin. I earned a BA in zoology in three years by taking classes year-round, while also working in the lab and holding down a part-time job. I thrived on being busy; indeed, I earned my highest grades when I carried the heaviest load.

For most of my undergraduate education, I was so busy with classes and work that, although I had decided to pursue a graduate degree, I had not thought about it in concrete terms. I had a vague notion of how one goes about selecting graduate programs and, once accepted into graduate programs, how one decides which one is best for him or her. This process seemed so abstract to me. One especially important set of decisions to make involved my area of specialization. Suddenly, I had to answer some very specific questions: What kinds of scientific questions fascinated me? Which graduate program and which university would best enable me to pursue my studies? I quickly came to the embarrassing realization that I still lacked a clear idea of what specific area of biology I wanted to study, and that I must take the time to read and think deeply about areas of interest. So, upon completing my degree, I enrolled in graduate school at the University of Texas, where I took graduate courses in developmental neurobiology and immunogenetics, served as a teaching assistant for a histology course, and thought hard about my future plans. Often, I wondered if I had the creativity and insight to design my own projects. Equally important, it became obvious to me that I was abysmally ignorant of the vast scientific literature on any given topic that interested me, and that a familiarity with that literature was essential to grasping the key, unsolved problems in a field. By attending seminars and through my graduate courses I gradually gained confidence in reading the primary scientific literature, learning how to interpret the data figures to understand the experiments, learning how to pose a scientific question, and figuring out how to choose the best experimental approach to solve a scientific problem. During that single year in graduate school in Austin, I went through an important transition: I began learning the craft of an independent scientist as opposed to that of a scientific technician.

During that year, I applied to graduate programs at Harvard, Yale, Stanford, the California Institute of Technology, and the University of Washington, Seattle (the latter out of deference to one of my University of Texas professors, who was a University of Washington alumnus). Caltech sent a rejection letter almost immediately. I was accepted at the other four institutions. I was disappointed by the Caltech rejection because I had read and was very impressed by a historical treatise on important questions in embryology and developmental biology written by a Caltech professor, Eric Davidson. (As fate would have it, our paths crossed twice again later in my education.) Now I had to decide where to pursue my graduate studies. Three University of Texas faculty members in particular gave invaluable guidance and insight. Professor Lawrence E. Gilbert discussed with me the many facets of graduate studies. Dr. George Bittner, who taught me developmental neurobiology, introduced me to Dr. Donald Kennedy, professor and future president of Stanford University, so that I might learn more about Stanford. (At the time that I was applying to graduate schools, it was not common practice for graduate programs to bring applicants to their campuses.) Dr. Bobby G. Sanders allowed me to work in his lab during that first year of graduate school and instilled in me an appreciation for the immune system. After consulting with these and other faculty members, I decided to go to Yale University, where I was admitted into the molecular, cell, and developmental biology program. In retrospect, I can appreciate the many wonderful aspects of that graduate program: the mentorship by the second-year students, the unobtrusive guidance of the director of graduate studies, Ian Sussex, the classical embryology course taught by three giants in that field. I decided to take my qualifying examinations a year early, with the second-year class, a bold and (some would say) insane move, but one that compelled me to read the scientific literature more deeply. I passed the exams! I also was awarded a four-year Ford Foundation predoctoral fellowship.

At the end of my first year of graduate school, I applied and was accepted to the embryology course at the Marine Biological

Laboratories in Woods Hole, Massachusetts, which was organized by Caltech's Eric Davidson. Woods Hole is a magical place in the summer. It teems with scientists who are there to work hard and discuss science at length in a beautiful environment. I was in heaven! The remainder of my graduate career was less idyllic. Along the way, I was confronted with problems as diverse as being denied admission into the lab that was my first choice, personality conflicts with the postdoc fellow with whom I worked in the lab that I did join, and being robbed at home and mugged in my own backyard. In an unexpected way, the mugging particularly eroded my self-confidence. I had entered graduate school confident and optimistic. I finished graduate school feeling demoralized and frightened. I applied for postdoctoral positions, but I was so devoid of self-esteem that I could not imagine actually taking one on. The adventurous girl who had boldly sallied forth from Texas to Connecticut was now fearful of venturing as far away as Cold Spring Harbor, on the south shore of Long Island.

> Oft expectation fails, and most oft there
> Where most it promises; and oft it hits
> Where hope is coldest, and despair most fits.
> —William Shakespeare, *All's Well That Ends Well*

After many unwise decisions, I finally found my way to a postdoctoral position that was appropriate for me, a stint in the laboratory of Leroy Hood at Caltech. The Ford Foundation postdoctoral fellowship supported me during my first year at Caltech, after which I was awarded a Cancer Research Institute three-year fellowship. Between the completion of my PhD and my first publication from the Hood lab lay a desolate six years or so during which I observed colleagues' careers shoot forth like meteors. I trudged and toiled with a tenacity that was double-dose, having been handed down in the genes I inherited through both my parents' lineages. Through it all, I tried to imagine a life outside of science, and I occasionally fantasized about a less demanding career, but I couldn't think of anything as enthralling as a research career. Science possessed me now, body and soul, and there was no desire for or possibility of escape. So, no matter how cold hope seemed at times, I knew that I would persevere. I would have a career in science, perhaps not a glorious one, perhaps not a glamorous one, but a career nonetheless, in which I would use my wits, my creativity, and my tenacity to mine for answers to the mysteries of life itself.

> Dance me to your beauty with a burning violin.
> Dance me through the panic 'til I'm gathered safely in.
> —Leonard Cohen, "Dance Me to the End of Love"

In pursuing my educational and career goals, I lived in nine different cities (two of them twice). In each city, I tried to create a home away from home by finding people and situations that nurtured me. When I failed to establish those moorings, I did not fare so well. My fellow Mexican American graduate students at Yale University complained about being far away from their home and their culture. I, on the other hand, felt privileged to be at Yale, and my overriding desire was to benefit maximally from my experience there. Of course, I missed my family. In particular, I was sad to miss watching my youngest brothers grow up, to be growing apart from my sisters, to see my family only once a year, and to be away from my grandparents as they entered the twilight of their lives. It was a struggle to remain part of my family and to maintain the bonds that had once seemed so strong. It gave me such joy to have my parents visit me in New Haven and come into the lab with me. I proudly introduced them to my fellow graduate students. My mother was fifty at the time and had mothered ten children. I recall with pleasure that one labmate remarked afterward on my mother's beauty. He said, "She is not only physically beautiful; she is beautiful within." This friend had assessed my mother so astutely in a matter of minutes.

> From the very day when a Zúñiga baby girl is born, she is taught the basic fundamentals of being a performer and a people-person. Her cousins and aunts show her how to point her chubby little toes and how to smile brightly. As her mentors, they work diligently to try and fill her with the passion and charisma the Zúñiga women all have.
>
> —Alli Hrncir (my cousin's daughter)

A popular misimpression of scientists, perpetuated by movies and television, is that we are socially dysfunctional nerds or psychotic maniacs, and, in either case, that we are out of touch with both the human soul and "the real world." The irony is that scientists study the real world, and those who are biologists study the very essence of life itself. Those of us who also teach must, by definition, be able to relate to people. I love the above excerpt from my cousin's sixteen-year-old daughter's essay on what it is to be a Zúñiga woman for two reasons. It relates so well the joy of being part of a large and loving family in which the girls and women mentor one another. Moreover, it reveals how girlhood in this family of mine, which emphasized dancing and the performing arts, gave me the grace and passion to venture forth, to seize the opportunities that others might have considered unavailable to me.

> May your hands always be busy,
> May your feet always be swift,
> May you have a strong foundation
> When the winds of changes shift.
>
> —Bob Dylan, "Forever Young"

Throughout my education and my career, my work has been a source of joy, satisfaction, and mental youthfulness. I love engaging in research projects of my own design, teaching new generations of students, and using my knowledge of immunology and virology to help my family when one of them confronts a medical problem. But one aspect of my career that was totally unexpected was the feeling that I am engaged in an endless uphill sprint, with few plateaus. In this regard, I have found it essential to rely on my strong foundations when, as Bob Dylan says, "the winds of changes shift."

> Sun setting in the west;
> my thoughts return to you,
> savoring what was best
> when we were one, not two.
>
> —Martha Zúñiga

When I was in graduate school, I fell in love with and married a fellow scientist. Actually, at the time, I was hesitant to marry because my beloved was further along in his career than I was, and I sensed it would be difficult for both of us to find jobs in the same city. Until I completed my degree, life was wonderful. Each morning, my husband and I went to our respective labs, and at the end of the day we met at the Payne Whitney gym on the Yale campus, exercised together, then went home for a romantic dinner. When I finished my PhD, I interviewed for postdoctoral positions in New York City and Cold Spring Harbor. Both of these options would have required that I commute on the train, something that neither my husband nor I found appealing. My husband knew I enjoyed writing and tried to persuade me to get a job working at the magazine of the Sigma Xi scientific society, which was published in New Haven at that time. I was torn. I wanted to participate in the craft of science, not write about it! The option of taking a postdoctoral position in either New York City or Cold Spring Harbor became completely unacceptable after the night I was mugged outside our home. That had a profoundly negative impact on me, eroding my self-confidence. After that, I stayed at home for a while, making drapes for the house, baking bread, and otherwise being the perfect wife. The only problem was that when my husband came home at night, he felt a need for the solitude of his study while I was starved for intellectual stimulation. I read scientific journals in the Yale University science library, where I would stare enviously at the busy people walking in and out. I proceeded to make a series of unwise decisions regarding my postdoctoral training. Then my husband took a sabbatical year at the California Institute of Technology, and there my career was relaunched. But still we were plagued by the impossible goal of finding jobs together, and the stress eventually destroyed our marriage.

One of my deepest regrets is not having had children, because I adore children and know I would have enjoyed being a mother. A significant problem that women in science must confront is when to have children: during graduate school, as soon as one earns the PhD, during one's postdoc years, as soon as one has an assistant professor position, after one is tenured? Before it dissolved, my marriage became a long-distance one, with my husband in New Haven and me three thousand miles away in Pasadena, California, a situation that was hardly conducive to becoming pregnant. With the benefit of hindsight, I think that I should have taken courage in hand and started a family as soon as I could, even if it would have diminished my career opportunities. At the time, however, I felt I would be failing in the eyes of the feminist movement, which exhorted young women such as me to pursue a career, and viewed being a wife and mother as not

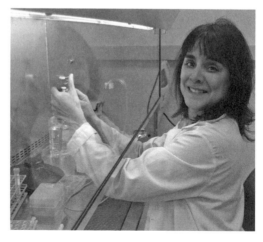

Martha Cecilia Zúñiga working in the lab, 2007.

being a complete woman. After all, Gloria Steinem remained single until she was about sixty years old! Now I have remarried, but we do not have children. Instead, I devote myself to my husband and to my parents, brothers, and sisters, and to their children. I strive to be a good aunt to my nephews and nieces, and to provide them with the loving mentorship that is sometimes more easily obtained from another adult than from one's parent.

> Well, the Lone Ranger and Tonto
> They are ridin' down the line
> Fixin' ev'rybody's troubles
> Ev'rybody's 'cept mine
> Somebody musta tol' 'em
> That I was doin' fine.
>
> —Bob Dylan, "Bob Dylan's Blues"

A career in academic science is very rewarding but also very demanding. A professor must be effective at teaching, research, raising funds to support the research program, and managing a research group, all while carrying out other faculty and professional duties. Many disappointments and setbacks arise, and at times it seems that one's career is in shambles. At times such as these, it can be difficult to muster the emotional and mental fortitude to seek and take advantage of the right combination of emotional support, mentoring, and luck that are essential to continue forging ahead. Certainly, there have been times when I have found myself in a seemingly hopeless situation, had difficulty summoning the courage and strength to continue, and felt too defeated to even ask for advice. For this reason, I have often thought that academic scientists need coaches and trainers at least as much as athletes do, and I have lamented the fact that each of us must find his or her own way. I am thus very committed to being a mentor to students and colleagues alike, to help them through the inevitable difficult times.

"What sort of things do *you* remember best?" Alice ventured to ask.
"Oh, things that happened the week after next," the Queen replied in a careless tone.
            —Lewis Carroll, *Through the Looking-Glass and What Alice Found There*

The Queen's response to Alice may seem nonsensical, but in its own way it constitutes apt advice for students who wish to pursue careers in science, math, or engineering. Imagining your future in science and then planning for it can be the key to opening doors. While you are in high school, imagine yourself in college, and while in college, imagine yourself in graduate school, and while in graduate school, imagine yourself in your future career, so that you may "remember" what will happen in that future stage in the wonderful life that unfolds before you. Of course, more than likely, your imaginings will not be realized in the same way that you thought, but they will set you on the path, particularly if you seek the guidance of mentors and the support of loved ones, friends, and colleagues.

Part III
Pasos con Veredas

CHAPTER 7

The Education of a Chicana Scientist

Elvia Elisa Niebla
Director of Global Change Research

*I*n the 1950s, living on the border meant you could cross the street and change countries. Since I had ancestors who had been born and had lived on both sides of the Mexican–U.S. border, my family had the choice of living on either side. For the first seven years of my life, we lived on the Mexican side; I finished first grade in the Mexican school system. At that time, my immediate family decided to live closer to my maternal grandmother, who lived on the U.S. side of the border. Almost literally we crossed the street and changed countries.

My parents also decided to move because their children would have access to better educational opportunities in the United States. Education has always been important to my family, and senior family members held high expectations for their children. In the U.S. school, I was enrolled initially into the kindergarten class to learn English. By then, I already knew how to read and write in Spanish. In kindergarten you do not actually learn to write in English, only how to form circles and hooks. I had that down pat from my previous schooling, so within a month I was promoted to the first grade. In elementary school, I always performed well and felt successful in my schoolwork. During the first month of sixth grade, my homeroom teacher (curiously, the only African American teacher left in our local school system since the abolition of segregated schools in my hometown), who knew I was performing ahead of my grade level, began the process of promoting me to the seventh grade; because of her interest and effort, I skipped another grade. These actions early in my life were certainly helpful in building my confidence and self-assurance, and fueling my hopes of attending college.

As I reminisce about my school years, I can now recall some anguished moments. For example, in elementary school, the teachers held competitions that were similar to spelling bees but covered several subjects. By lining up members of each classroom along the walls, classrooms would compete against each other; questions pertaining to the various class subjects—history, geography, and, of course, spelling—would be asked of each class member in turn. If the student gave the wrong answer, she or he would sit down and the questioning would continue until all the members of one classroom were seated. The classroom that had at least one student standing won. I believe that students were tracked at that time, because it was obvious that the smarter kids were in Class A and the others were in Class B. The students in Class A were mostly Anglo, English speaking, and wealthier. In contrast, the students in Class B were usually Chicano children who spoke English as a second language and tended to be poor. During class competitions, most of the students in Class B would soon be seated, unable to answer the questions correctly. Although I was a Chicana student in Class B, I studied the questions and would

often be one of the last left
standing from my class
after a couple of rounds.
Sometimes I would be the
sole student answering
questions against fifteen or
twenty students from Class
A. While I was standing
alone, I felt my classmates
cheering me on, hoping
I would win; my victory
was their victory, too. Even
though I enjoyed the victo-
ries, I was deeply aware
of the embarrassment my
classmates felt when they

Elvia Elisa Niebla with her family, 1948.

did not know the right answers. When I won for our classroom, it was
as if all of us were vindicated, because I was one of them.

Later, during my middle school and high school years, whenever
we had special testing days for college prep, the Mexican students did
not participate in the same proportions, even though there was a high
percentage of Mexican American kids in the classroom. It appeared
as though these students were not expected to go to college. This
assumption always perplexed me, because I felt many of them were
at least as capable as I was and could have succeeded. Instead, the
system retained and met only marginal expectations of these students.
In fact, a very small number of my schoolmates did attend college.

Language Issues: Dos Lenguas

As a Chicana living in a border town, I grew up with relatives on both sides of the border. This biculturalism extended beyond the border. My maternal grandmother, Bertha Rankin, was a U.S. citizen of European ancestry; in fact, she was first-generation Czechoslovakian, and married my stepgrandfather, Charles D. Rankin, who did not speak a word of Spanish. In contrast, my father's relatives came from a long line of teachers in Mexico and did not speak English. As a matter of fact, my father's maternal grandfather, José María Gómez (that is, my great-grandfather), was sent in the late nineteenth century by the Mexican government to the border with a group of fellow teachers to combat illiteracy at the frontier of the country. While I was growing up, I was instructed by my father's siblings, who were all teachers living on the Mexican side and who were monolingual Spanish speakers. We spoke Spanish with them and would be corrected if we did not speak it correctly. As a consequence, I grew up bilingual; to communicate with my loved ones, I had to know both Spanish and English.

Knowing two languages has always been a source of joy and pride. Whenever I visited Mexico City, I attended a theater performance almost every night with my aunts, who were aficionados. Since it is such a big city, there were plenty of theater and live performances, so many that one could see at least ten different shows within a two-week vacation. There were performances at Blanquita Theater, and plays such as *La Vida Es Solo un Sueño* by Calderon de la Barca, and even musicals, such as *Vaselina* or *Evita*. I thoroughly enjoyed these outings in Spanish. Then, in the United States, I could see Shakespeare's plays, such as *Julius Caesar* and *King Lear*, in their original language. One advantage of being bilingual is that you can enjoy and appreciate English and Spanish literature in their original composition. However, being a bilingual person has not always been rewarded or acknowledged as an asset.

Because I am bilingual, throughout my career I have been asked to help with translations. This ability has opened many doors and has given me access, which I might not have otherwise had, to people in authority. For example, in my first year as a graduate student, the department chair, Dr. Barnes, had to visit a university in Mexico, and I was invited to accompany him on this trip. During our travel I developed a wonderful friendship with him; I acquired his respect, and he began to take an interest in my graduate program.

Other opportunities for translating presented themselves. Because the University of Arizona, my alma mater, was only sixty miles north of the Mexican border, Spanish translation was frequently needed since we often had visitors from Mexico. It was an easy task for me, and I always felt privileged that my dual language abilities came in handy. Later, in Washington DC, officials from Mexico, such as the counterpart to our secretary of agriculture, visited the chief of the Forest Service (an agency of the U.S. Department of Agriculture) and I would serve as the intermediary, translating for both of them. I wanted to do the translating, and I made excellent friends both here and internationally, such as in Mexico and Canada. I enjoyed such experiences enormously.

In spite of the wonderful connections I made with people, such as the chief of the Forest Service, my translation responsibilities never appeared on the list of duties considered for merit promotion or merit increases. I worked extra hours without acknowledgment or additional compensation for my linguistic skills. In fact, this asset was unappreciated and undervalued by individuals on the Forest Service international staff. Once, a scientific paper needed to be translated for a United Nations publication, and I suggested that another Chicano scientist assist in the translation. The international affairs individual interjected and said that Chicanos did not speak Spanish correctly, insinuating that they were all _pochos_ (Chicanos who spoke poor Spanish). This individual had never spoken Spanish with me or with the scientist I had recommended. I did not contest the issue, so the translation work was contracted out for thousands of dollars. Ironically, the translated paper was unacceptable and was sent to me for corrections. The paper had gone to a translator recommended by the State Department, an English speaker who knew some Spanish but was unfamiliar with scientific terms. I felt vindicated, but still I did the work without additional recognition.

Being bilingual has created extra work throughout my career. During my graduate school years, I realized that having clear diction in English was another asset that could create obstacles. Toward the completion of my doctorate, I was granted a research fellowship so that I could dedicate all my efforts to my research and write my dissertation during the fall semester. However, a week before the semester began, the professor in charge of assigning teaching responsibilities informed me that the students from the Middle East who had teaching scholarships could not speak English clearly enough to teach; since I was such a good teacher, my appointment would be changed from a research to a teaching fellowship. Since my advisor was out of town, the transaction took place without giving him an opportunity to protest and protect my time for research.

Later, during my working career, I became aware of a similar situation in grant funding from federal agencies in Washington DC. In an effort to increase the number of minorities in the sciences, the program managers encouraged the employment of minority students in research grants. However, universities often give research fellowships to foreign students who might not know English well enough to teach. Thus, the Chicana/o or native-born minorities are required to do the teaching, making it difficult to build their résumés with research publications.

Guardian Angels: *Familia, Amigos, y Conocidos*

According to my life recollections, I never had large obstacles to over-come. I consider myself a very lucky individual. However, as I analyze my situation, I realize that it was not only luck but also "guardian angels" who helped eliminate obstacles as I approached various cross-roads. These guardian angels came in the form of family members as well as strangers. Although my family never accumulated savings to send us to college, take us on vacations, or provide other luxuries, the family income was sufficient to eke out a comfortable living. Despite this fact, I always expected I would go to college somehow. Soon after my high school graduation in May, my brother, Fernando, who had been married just over a year and was established in California, arrived at our home in Arizona with his young wife and my first niece. It had been decided that I would live with him at no expense and attend Fullerton Junior College near his home. I do not recall discussing this or being asked about the matter. But I was happy to be going to college, and although I had never heard of junior colleges, I enrolled at Fullerton Junior College and loved every minute of it.

I have always felt very grateful for the gifts I was given by my brother and his wife, Olga, especially the gift of time and the freedom from financial concerns while I attended junior college. My brother, who had just graduated himself as an electrical engineer, knew the importance of having a study area at home. He arranged a desk and space in his home office for me. My only responsibilities were to bring in the garbage cans on Mondays for my brother and wash the daily dinner dishes to help my sister-in-law. There were no other expecta-tions; I was on my own. My dad, who had never before written to me, started sending me letters with spending money. In high school my big dream had been to go away to school, so I was entirely pleased that I was attending a junior college in California. Although my basic living expenses were covered, there was no money for luxuries such as new clothes or a car, but I felt no necessity to work. Not working was a good choice, because my first years in college proved to be quite demanding due to my lack of preparation. The science laboratories in my small town's only high school were very limited, and I was not prepared for the advanced college science classes required of chemistry and zoology majors. We did not even have calculus courses in my high school. But fortunately, my rudimentary preparation was solid.

I gained advanced math preparation from my high school algebra professor, Mr. Summers, who made himself available after school to work with me on special projects. One day, after passing out the algebra exam results to the class, he did not return my paper and instead asked me to see him after school. I was terrified; I wondered what had gone wrong with the exam. Could I have failed? No—he simply wanted to congratulate me on my work and offer to help me after school with extra math projects, since more advanced math classes were not offered at the school. Thus he, too, became a guardian angel, eliminating unseen obstacles in my path. Mr. Summers, a nondescript man as far as I was concerned, made a special effort and gave me his time so that I would learn to enjoy math outside the classroom. He helped prepare me for the higher mathematics expected of college students.

However, not even the special attention from Mr. Summers prepared me for the demanding science courses in college. I felt that no matter how hard I tried, I could not make the straight A's I was used to in high school. Now I realize how fortunate I was to maintain a respectable grade point average, given the gaps in my earlier educational experience.

In my third year of college, I transferred to the University of Arizona without losing a single credit hour from my junior college courses. By this point, I felt I was finally on par with my fellow students; I realized that the education I had gotten during the previous two years made it possible for me to comprehend the lectures and understand the material I had to study to ace an organic chemistry class. I would receive 140 points, including extra points in the exams, when the class average was 30 to 40 points. I enjoyed organic chemistry. For me, working with organic reactions and recombining carbon chains was like doing puzzles. My grades placed me at the top of the class. I was the same person putting in the same amount of effort, but now I had excellent grades as well. I felt euphoric. I mention this to emphasize the importance of acquiring the foundation to tackle classes that appear difficult due to the lack of a solid background in the subject. Often, smart Chicana/o students do not perform well due to limited high school preparation.

Another discouraging experience, due not to lack of ability but to lack of academic instruction, was my performance in various physics classes. I took the physics exams and solved the problems using algebra. Although I was able to find the right answers, I never had enough time to answer all the questions. I could not figure out how others could finish the exams. Once I took a course in differential equations, I acquired the tool I needed to solve the physics problems quickly, since differential equations used fewer steps than algebra. I was finally able to complete the exams. Indeed, having the right foundational courses made it possible to perform well.

I have many Chicana friends who tell me that they would have studied chemistry, math, or physics if the courses had not been so hard. I know that many of these people are smart and that the principles of science are not impossible to learn if the task is taken a step at a time. Scientific principles are so much easier to learn with a sound fundamental base. I have learned you can climb to the top of the ladder only by stepping on the bottom rungs first, one at a time. A strong foundation in mathematics is essential for students wishing to pursue college degrees in science and engineering.

The first semester after I transferred to the university in 1965, my father covered all my expenses. During that semester, my father suffered a sudden death. In spite of the great changes my family faced, I felt supported. My older sister, María Elena, assumed the household responsibilities and never considered the possibility of interrupting my education. I continued and registered for the second semester, hoping the money would materialize somehow. On the final day to pay registration fees, the money had still not surfaced. Prior to going to the registrar's to discuss my circumstances, I walked to the post office, where to my surprise I was rescued once again. Two letters were in the mail: my brother had sent a check for four hundred dollars to cover my registration and dorm rent, and my sister had arranged for monthly allotments from my father's insurance to be sent during the duration of my time in school.

My family members were not the only ones easing the path for me. Along my journey, other individuals have made a difference sometimes unbeknownst to me! The same day that I received those timely letters, after paying my school fees, I inquired about the work-study program. The individual I had to request information from was a six-foot-tall, heavy-set man with a goatee and mustache. His demeanor was altogether off-putting and austere. But I braced myself, stated my circumstances, and requested a job. While this is simple to tell now, at the time it was quite an ordeal. It was soon after my dad's funeral, and the first occasion on which I had to explain my father's passing. To my chagrin, I broke down and started crying. I was very embarrassed but also tremendously grateful that this man did not bat an eye, as if students broke down in his office every day. He filled out a form and told me to go to an office in the zoology department. I was a little perplexed and inquired when I would know if I had a job. He replied very matter-of-factly, "You already have a job, and if it doesn't work out, come see me again." During the rest of my academic career I had the occasion to communicate with him only once or twice, when he called to ask how I was doing in my job. Years later, while I was pursuing graduate work, I saw him on campus; I was sure he did not recognize me. Even later, I was invited back to the university as a guest speaker in the career-day program. This man was also one of the participants, and as I was introduced to him, he beamed and said that he knew me very well indeed and that he had been following my progress all along. He was impressed with my presentation and complimented me on my presence as a working scientist. He was about to retire and my achievements had made him tremendously proud; he remembered me as a frightened kid who was at a loss for words many years ago in his office, and he knew he had made a difference. For over sixteen years, I had been under the impression that the austere man with a mustache and goatee who had witnessed my embarrassing break-down had not even noticed my presence. Now he was telling me that my accomplishments had given meaning to his life's work.

Finding a Path: Haciendo Camino

At an early age, I started to show signs of curiosity and inquisitiveness. My mother was very supportive and encouraged such behavior, which led me to choose science as my life's work. Science was not just inter-esting to me; I also had an altruistic goal fostered by the impression that, as a scientist, one could contribute to the general well-being of society. At the time, I considered becoming a research scientist. But I was uncertain as to what specific field of science I would pursue. Through exposure to the different fields, I narrowed my PhD major to soil chemistry. As my career progressed, I saw the need to develop my management skills to direct a research laboratory, so I also completed a master of science in business administration. Later, when I accepted a position in Washington DC, I used my scientific background to advise policy makers on environmental regulations and other science policies, and used my management degree in my role as an administrator. During this time, I had the opportunity to attend Harvard University as a senior executive fellow; later, as a Brookings Institution fellow, I was a staffer for Congressman Ed Pastor of Arizona. I loved these fascinating experiences, but I would not have imagined them as career choices when I first chose to become a scientist. To understand these career choices, let's start at the beginning.

As a kid, I loved the outdoors and spent most of my free time climbing trees and playing in the hills of Nogales. My mother was probably the most influential person in nurturing my curiosity and ideas. At four, when I jumped out of a tree, trying to fly like Superman, instead of forbidding my imaginary exploits, she made a towel into a Superman cape, hoping that it would satisfy my desire to play the hero's role, although I could not fly. At seven, I wanted to paint my white dog pink; she suggested we bathe him in food coloring, and I got a pink dog just like I wanted. At ten, I came home with a "fish" from a puddle in the arroyo. Mom set up a glass bottle so I could watch him develop legs and become a frog. It had been a tadpole, not a fish, but Mom had shown me, not told me, and in this way I learned many lessons. Certainly these experiences must have impelled my inquisitive mind toward science. My mother fostered my natural curiosity and never once made me feel as though my ideas were silly or unimportant.

My questions were not always easy to answer, at least judging from the reaction of my elders. I distinctly remember the day I learned about Darwin's theory of evolution and how we were related to the chimpanzee. I was about seven or eight years old, and had thus far only learned about creation by God through Adam and Eve in our catechism class. At the time, I wanted an explanation of the correlation between Darwin's theory and the story of Adam and Eve in the Bible. The question, of course, was posed to the person I thought knew everything, or at least a lot more than I, my twelve-year-old sister, María Elena. As usual, she did not wince at the question and guided me to an answer, never letting on that my question was unreasonable. She sent me first to the parish priest, but admonished that I should not be satisfied with his answer. I was then to go to my science teacher, Mr. García, with the same question. Thus my immediate family usually took my questions seriously and attempted to respond to my curiosity.

Although my mother and family were extremely supportive, they did not condone all of my experiments. On one Halloween, I arrived at the idea that by surprising as many senses as possible at a single moment, I could frighten someone to the nth degree. I decided to test my idea on my unsuspecting sister, Bertha, who was closest to my age and who was also my closest playmate. As she entered our bedroom, I turned the light switch off, threw a stinky rag at her, and yelled, thus covering four senses. My experiment was a great success; Bertha cried out, nearly fainted, and was traumatized for a long while. My mother was outraged, but worst of all, I felt terrible and worried that my sister would never stop crying or shaking. Early in my college years, I took a course in the history of science, where we were introduced to the age-old philosophical argument of the responsibility of the scientist for his or her actions and inventions. I thought back on this incident as my first experience of this concept. As I have mentioned, the social contribution a scientist can make was an important factor in my career choice; thus these philosophical discussions further encouraged me to proceed along the path of science.

Because of my love of animals, I chose to major in zoology and minor in chemistry as an undergraduate. At this time, I also got a work-study job in the zoology department, stuffing birds as a taxidermist for the museum. Due to the demands of my job and several of my laboratory courses, I spent all my waking hours in the zoology building. Because the specimens were preserved in formaldehyde, the building reeked from the fumes, and my senses could not withstand it. In contrast, I loved the immaculate cleanliness of the analytical chemistry laboratories and was fascinated by the exactness of the science. I was intrigued that when given an unknown, I could take a small amount, expose it to a number of given chemical reactions, and not only identify the elements present, such as calcium or magnesium, but also determine the minutest amount present. So I enrolled in analytical chemistry for graduate work and was given a lab assistant job in a soil science laboratory. As time passed, the professor in charge of the

lab, Dr. Dutt, warned me he would convince me to become his student in soil chemistry. I became an associate researcher in a project sponsored by the Environmental Protection Agency (EPA) that investigated how soil could abate or filter contaminants in sewage water. The project entailed a specific use of analytical chemistry and seemed practical, as it addressed everyday

Elvia Elisa Niebla collecting soil samples in Death Valley, California, circa 1980.

problems. With this research, we could learn to protect our environment and keep it safe for living organisms. From this experience I
realized exactly what kind of scientist I wanted to be—a soil scientist.

My first job after completing my PhD was with the National Park
Service in the Western Archeological Center. This was a terrific job
experience; I was actually paid to visit the national parks in the West,
an activity that I had previously chosen for vacations. Part of my job
responsibility was to perform chemical analyses on prehistoric and
historic adobe buildings to determine the soils used in their construction. Often, I located the sites—called barro pits—where the soil was
originally dug out for use in making the adobe bricks. Another aspect
of the job was to make the Western Archeological Laboratory pay for
itself. Thus, I had to determine the cost of the analysis in terms of
materials, equipment, and laboratory personnel. These analyses were
not chemically based; one needed skills for administering a business, which had not been provided in my science training. That is
why I decided to study business administration, eventually earning my
master of science in business administration.

During this period, the graduate work I had done for the EPA on
the abatement of pollutants from water was first appearing in the
scientific literature. Furthermore, the EPA was trying to find uses for
the large amounts of waste being generated by the Clean Water Act.
Although water was being filtered and cleaned before it was returned
to the rivers, the waste or sludge being filtered was accumulating, and
disposal of such waste needed to be regulated. The EPA offered me a
job to help develop regulations for the application of sludge to soils.
Even though I loved the West and had hoped to stay in the area, I
agreed to move to Washington DC for this work, since it matched
my experience and graduate research so well. The fit was so good, in
fact, that one of the first papers published by our staff for this project

was a coauthored publication of mine. I was also very pleased to join the EPA's mission and its efforts to clean the environment. The fact that the EPA was hiring scientists for its work was very encouraging; however, after arriving in Washington, I found that the attorneys and policy makers still held sway.

My job at the EPA was to calculate the amount of pollutants in the sludge that could be applied to soil without detrimentally affecting the environment. These calculations were done by using formulas and scouring the scientific literature for experimental results. Our findings were then presented to the policy makers, who would take this information, consider other factors such as economic impacts and prevailing political winds, and determine the pollutant levels permitted by the regulations. On the one hand, the job was frustrating because as a scientist I would have chosen to give more weight to the scientific facts than to the economic and political impacts; however, the endeavor was worthwhile because the resulting regulations did take into account some scientific truths.

My next assignment was in the Forest Service as the national global change research coordinator. My function was to coordinate the research on global change conducted by Forest Service researchers; our work included investigations concerning the ozone layer, global warming, deforestation, desertification, carbon sequestration, and other similar research. As the national coordinator, I also represented the Forest Service in the U.S. Global Change Research Program (USGCRP). This program was established when global change was recognized as a problem by the U.S. government; the government created this program instead of creating an agency, in contrast to its organizing the National Aeronautic and Space Administration (NASA) for space exploration. USGCRP handled relevant research projects that were best performed under the mission of several departments and agencies, such as the EPA, NASA, the Department of Energy, the National Science Foundation, the Department of the Interior, and the National Oceanic and Atmospheric Administration (NOAA). For example, while NOAA was better equipped to determine climate changes, the Forest Service was in a position to study the effects of climate change on forests. The Department of State was also part of this program, because they had to negotiate climate change issues at the international level, such as at the Environmental Summit in Brazil and at the Kyoto Protocol in Japan. Again, the scientists in the program provided the information for the policy makers, who made the agreements at the level of the United Nations.

These responsibilities provided tremendous opportunities for travel, since I had to visit the Forest Service scientists' projects implemented throughout the United States. After being on the job for a few years, I realized I had been to every state in the country except South Dakota and North Dakota. The travel was not limited to North America and included intercontinental destinations as well. Some of the most memorable trips included traveling to East Berlin soon after the Berlin Wall was torn down, and visiting the Black Forest in Austria, as well as attending a United Nations-sponsored meeting in Brazil. During my first job with the Park Service, I traveled the United States working at national parks; now, with the Forest Service, I traveled the world visiting world forests.

Extensive travel was not the only benefit reaped from my jobs with the U.S. government; I also had great opportunities to pursue additional training. As a long-term government employee, I was always supported and encouraged to take courses. My supervisor for ten years, Dr. Bill Sommers, particularly encouraged me. He always supported activities that widened my horizons and made me more effective in my position. One of the most interesting and beneficial experiences was taking a course on how to handle the media—that is, what one should say and do when approached by reporters, and how to give speeches and perform in front of TV cameras. As an employee of the executive branch, it was imperative to work with the legislative branch, especially to promote a budget favorable to the research program. Consequently, I was selected to attend the Senior Executive Fellows Program for a semester at the John F. Kennedy School of Government at Harvard University. The program was based on case studies of the way government functions. It was a wonderful experience, especially because it coincided with Bill Clinton's first presidential campaign, and all the candidates for the primaries came to Harvard during their campaigns. As students, we were able to attend small conferences not only with the Harvard faculty, which included politicians like Michael Dukakis, but also with all the prominent politicians of the time who came through and lectured at Harvard and the Massachusetts Institute of Technology.

Another training experience was serving as a Brookings Fellow on Capitol Hill. Under this program, we attended special seminars held at the Brookings Institution on current events, and spent eight months on the staff of a member of Congress. I chose to apply for a position with Congressman Ed Pastor, the representative of my hometown, Nogales, Arizona. Although he already had a staffer in charge of science issues, he offered me the opportunity to assist on science issues and be in charge of education and Latino issues, since I knew the language and culture. This was an exhilarating experience; I had the responsibility of attending weekly meetings with the Hispanic Caucus, which included about twenty Latina/o members of Congress who discussed issues of imminent importance to the nation's Latino community. Many times I had to stand in for the congressman and receive visitors from his district because he had to attend to a vote on the House floor; doing so allowed me to witness firsthand that citizens do have a voice in Congress through their representatives.

As a staffer, I also kept track of requests submitted to the congressman. In spring 1997, a proposal to award Mother Teresa the Congressional Gold Medal came to the congressman's office. Congress awards these medals as its highest expression of national appreciation for distinguished achievements and contributions. All requests for a Congressional Gold Medal must be cosponsored by two-thirds of the members of the House and by at least sixty-seven senators before the authorizing committee will consider them. I was pleased to bring this legislation to the attention of the congressman, and of course he immediately signed it. Later in the summer, I saw Mother Teresa arrive at the Capitol to receive her award. I believe that was the last trip she made to the United States; she died that September. Aside from all the experience and knowledge of legislation I gained by being a staffer on Capitol Hill, witnessing this event was one of the most special privileges I enjoyed.

Washington Living: Viviendo la Vida Buena

As much as I enjoyed working as a scientist in Washington DC, living there was also exhilarating. The city offered great entertainment, museums, historical sites, and nearby side trips, such as visits to New York, Annapolis, and Jamestown. I had the opportunity to widen my circle of interests to include fine art appreciation. I often spent weekends at the Smithsonian museums, developing interests far removed from science. I had the opportunity to see many special art exhibits and plays, and even to nurture a developing interest in spiritual matters. Many religion courses were offered at area schools, such as Catholic, Georgetown, and Trinity universities. I took advantage of some of these offerings and enrolled at Georgetown University in a certificate program in spirituality, which exposed me to enthralling lectures by the faculty, many of whom were Jesuit priests. This program, as well as other meditation courses, taught me meditative practices that I exercise daily.

In Washington I was also able to feed my hunger for dramatic performances. Living close to the Arena Stage theater complex, a resident theater, made it convenient to become a volunteer for the arts. I performed the duties of hostess for opening night receptions held for the press and actors' families. I attended the parties and not only met the actors but also received free tickets for the performances. For the longest time, I was able to attend every single performance presented in the complex. I loved it, for I saw top actors in the nation perform classic and avant-garde theater pieces.

Washington DC also offered me many opportunities to attend political and arts-related receptions. Some of the most memorable, of course, were the presidential inaugurations and inaugural balls. Foreign embassies often held receptions for their national artists or artisans in an attempt to introduce their national cultures to the DC area. During Hispanic Heritage Month, most of the departments and agencies also offered special functions. One such function was the presentation of the paintings of Jesse Treviño, an artist from San Antonio, at the American Art Musem. Major celebrations included events at the Kennedy Center for the Hispanic Heritage Awards, where I met Jimmy Smits and Gloria Estefan, and events at Washington University's Lisner Auditorium for the National Endowment for the Arts Heritage Awards, where I met the famed accordion player from San Antonio, Santiago Jimenez, and Cuban cellist Cachao. In addition, many popular authors frequently came to Washington for readings. That is how I became friends with outstanding Chicana authors such as Sandra Cisneros, Norma Cantú, Ana Castillo, Gloria Anzaldúa, and Denise Chávez. I also had the opportunity to meet artists in both the music and art worlds, such as Carmen Lomas Garza and Tish Hinojosa. Living in Washington was wonderful, not only because of my work but also because the city offers a wonderful, exciting cultural life.

In 2005, I was on assignment at Texas A&M Corpus Christi, assisting the dean of the Department of Science and Technology in acquiring funding from federal agencies. At the completion of this assignment, I retired from the federal government. I have loved the life of a scientist; it's been a trajectory full of wonder and awe. I cannot fathom what life would have been like had I made a different career choice. My wish is that this brief autobiography will encourage other Chicanas to imagine themselves as scientists and pursue their heart's desire.

CHAPTER 8

Aprendiendo a Vivir

Elsa Cantú Ruíz
*Assistant Professor of
Mathematics Education*

*F*or years I woke up to the smell of coffee. Every day since I can remember, Dad would get up early and make the coffee. He would then call us to get up and get dressed for school. Because my siblings and I had to share the one and only bathroom in the house, he would call us one at a time. I am the fourth child in a family of eleven children—eight sisters and three brothers. Mom often recalls the time she took us to visit Dad's relatives in Monterrey around the holidays; the owner of a lunch stand in Sabinas, a small town between Nuevo Laredo and Monterrey, where we stopped for soft drinks, asked her if she had invited all the neighborhood kids. She remembers also that for several years every Sunday we would fill a whole pew at San Luis Rey Church. Yes, we were quite a family. And like most, we were brought up with joys and sorrows.

In 1968, when the conflict in Asia had escalated to a horrible war, my brother Tino was killed in Vietnam. I recall the day the news came.

157

Early one February morning, a couple of men in uniform knocked at our door. Dad was already up, because I could smell the coffee when we received the news about my brother's death. Recently, my mother told me that even before answering the door she knew. I think that is the worst news parents can receive. Mom shares that she was still in bed and had peeked out the window, and when she saw the men climbing out of the army-green Volkswagen, she knew then and there. I think parents know these things in their hearts. My brother's death was very hard on Mom. Her heart was broken. I remember she cried for days, mostly to herself, and even years later she would cry unexpectedly. I called them her silent tears: never making a big *escándalo*, not letting everyone know, but mourning and missing my brother in her heart and in her own unvoiced manner. But I remember my dad's reaction most of all. Until then I believed that men did not cry. That day in February was the first time I saw my father cry. How hard it was for him to continue and go on with his life. It must have been the hardest thing he endured in his eighty-seven years. He blamed God, and I remember him cursing angrily and hitting the wall that morning. And when the priest from the neighborhood church came by later that day, Dad was angry with him, too. During the days between receiving the news and the wake, my father aged, and the hazel green of his eyes turned a sad gray. If sadness were a color, my dad's eyes had turned that color. Dad's picture was in the newspaper; the photo was taken as he was handed the triangular-folded U.S. flag that had draped my brother's coffin. My dad's face etched in that photo was sadder than I had ever seen it then or since. But eight daughters and two sons remained, and somehow my parents picked up the pieces and kept on going and raised their family.

Several days after my brother's funeral, I had to return to school. I was glad because I never liked missing school, and things at home

Elsa Cantú Ruíz, 1957.

were not quite the same anyway. There was so much sadness, and even though Mom tried, I could tell that it was different now. So when I went back to school, I did not ask Mom to write an excuse for me. I figured that when I told the lady in the office that I had been absent because my brother died, she would understand. Much to my surprise, the woman in charge of absence slips not only did not understand but also scolded me for being absent. And when I told her about my brother, she answered, *"Ya hasta los hermanos estan matando,"* alluding to how students always claimed that their grandmother had died, and now even brothers were dying. I left her office and went back home. I stayed out from school two more days and finally went back with a written note from home and a guarantee from Dad that he would go to school if the lady said anything to me again. I do not remember Dad having to go to school, so I must have been given the absence slip without further incident.

At home, Spanish was the only language spoken. So I spoke only Spanish when I entered first grade. I looked forward to going to school, but when I started school without knowing English, I was faced with a harsh reality. My three older siblings had all attended Saunders Elementary. My oldest sister, Norma, was in the sixth grade when I, too, started school at Saunders Elementary, a small four-classroom neighborhood school that housed grades first, second, and third. I often wondered if my siblings had managed to not use Spanish while at school, and how they had done it. The school was three blocks from my house, and we walked home for lunch every day. Always we had beans and tortillas and usually some kind of *sopa*, either *fideo* or *arroz*, with Kool-Aid or tea to drink.

I was very eager to start school. I loved seeing my older brother and sisters with their new school supplies, doing homework or reading, and speaking mostly English among themselves. I knew Spanish, but now I wanted–no, I needed–to learn English to be able to understand their conversations. They laughed when watching TV shows in English, even though that was rare, because the TV was mostly tuned to a Spanish channel and playing either *telenovelas* (soap operas) or a Mexican movie or program. *Gutierritos* was my favorite *telenovela*, and I would sit every afternoon glued to the TV. On the nights when Mom went to bingo with her *comadres* and Dad was at a softball game at Cruz Field or playing checkers with his friend Escamilla at Escamilla's gas station, Norma or Tino would turn the TV to an English channel. I wanted to learn English, but when I got to school I wanted to speak Spanish and was not allowed to; then I would want to speak English but did not know how. I was even punished for speaking Spanish in class. How was I to learn English without using my Spanish? School was certainly not what I had expected.

Dad and Mom knew little if any English. Although Mom was born in Corpus Christi, she had been raised in Mexico. Even though they both had little schooling (neither finished grade school), they placed a high value on their children's education. They always made sure we had school supplies and any necessary materials for school projects and programs. Mom would put school clothes on lay-away early in the summer so that we would have a new outfit to wear when the school year started. My older siblings worked picking cotton in the *pizcas* (the fields) during the summer months. The *pizcas* were a good way to earn the money needed for school supplies before school began. When I was old enough to join my older siblings, I was allowed to go to the *pizcas*, too. I felt grown up then but soon realized the work was not as much fun as I had thought. It was difficult work, and no matter how hard I tried filling up the sack there was always room for more cotton. Even though times were tough and we were poor, I never felt poor or felt I lacked anything. At times when Dad was laid off and out of work, I remember the priest or a church helper delivering bags of groceries to our house. I also recall accompanying Mom to get cheese, powdered milk, or whatever else the government was giving out that month. It was common in the neighborhood for families to receive such staples. In fact, I thought everybody got this help. It was not until I was in junior high school that I realized that my new friends' families did not receive assistance from the government; I figured that was so because their fathers had good jobs and even some of the mothers worked. It must have been especially hard on my parents during Christmases when Dad was laid off. However, they always managed, and every year we got the much-wanted doll or toy truck. And of course Mom would sew new dresses for us to wear for church on Christmas morning.

My brother Tino had quit school to join the army in April of his senior year, one month shy of graduation. Nevertheless, my dad was enormously proud because ten of his children graduated from Martin High School. For him that was a huge accomplishment. Even though he was not easily convinced that his daughters needed a college education, he was always quick to show how proud he was of those of us who got one. When my youngest sister, Geri, graduated from the University of Texas, Austin, Dad attended her graduation and painfully climbed the high stairs to a seat where he could not even distinguish her from the other graduates. He nonetheless stood up and proudly clapped when the ceremony was over, knowing that his youngest daughter had just graduated from *la universidad*.

It had been very different when his oldest daughter, Norma, wanted to go off to college. He refused because he did not understand the need for a daughter to have a college degree. After one year she had to quit school and work at a utility company. However, as the years went by, and with Mom's urging, Dad began to see the importance of a college education for all his children, including his daughters. After several years at the utility company, Norma quit her job and left town to get a degree. By the time I received my master's degree, and his youngest daughter, Geri, received her bachelor's degree, he might not have fully understood, but he was very *orgulloso*, very proud. When my son, Nono, my daughter, Klariza, or any of his grandchildren enrolled in college, he would pray to San Juan Bosco. He would say, *"Le pido a San Juan Bosco, el santo de los estudiantes, para que les vaya bien en los estudios."* He asked San Juan Bosco to help them with their studies. It took a long time for him to understand that high school was good, but that a college degree was an even greater accomplishment. At the age of eighty-seven, knowing that his days were not many and bidding his last farewell to me, he said, *"No dejes el doctorado,"* asking me not to quit graduate school and to get my PhD.

Unlike my dad, who did not understand the importance of an education beyond high school, Mom was always very supportive. She allowed us to study even if dishes needed to be washed. Sometimes she tried helping us with our homework, although it must have been hard for her because she did not know English. When I returned to college to get my degree, she cared for my son, Nono. It was easier for me to study or go to class knowing Mom would take good care of him. She never hesitated when I asked and always offered to help when she knew I needed time to complete a project or study for a test. By the time I was in graduate school and I needed to spend summers away from home to establish residency at the university, she looked after Klariza. Mom knew that education was essential, especially for her daughters, if her dreams for her children to get ahead in life were to be realized.

Early Schooling

My earliest recollection of school is of Mrs. Kirkpatrick, my first-grade teacher (there were no Head Start or prekindergarten programs then), and how she assigned pages and pages of *palitos y bolitas* (sticks and balls), a penmanship exercise. After a couple of days of this exercise, I approached her desk and told her, in my very broken English, that I wanted to write words and learn to read. I wanted to learn English. She said something like, "You are not ready for those yet," and sent me back to my desk. I obeyed, went back to my desk, and drew bigger *bolitas y palitos* to cover the page faster.

Soon after that I became bored with school and started receiving red D's in conduct. My father was furious with my first red D and went to school to *reclamar* (complain) and ask why the teacher did not like me, which is the explanation I had given him. But when Dad arrived, he saw that I was out of my seat, *platicando* (talking) with all my neighborhood friends, Diana, Tencha, Gera, Narciso, Leonel, and Macario. Mrs. Kirkpatrick explained that my desk was in the front of the classroom, next to her desk, because she needed to keep an eye on me, but that usually I was out of my seat *platicando* with my friends. He used to tell this story, emphasizing how embarrassed he felt, but Mom would say, "She takes after your side of the family." What could he say?

School was not a particularly good experience for me in the early grades. I do not remember much more about first or second grade except recess and gathering under the big cedar ash trees we called *cubrevientos*, and being kids in Spanish because inside the classroom we were not allowed to speak Spanish. When I was in third grade, my teacher, Mrs. Solis, finally sat with me and taught me how to read with comprehension. I was very excited, and my love of reading was born. I remember her sounding out the word *comfortable*, which I was having a hard time pronouncing. She also made reading come to life for me. I still remember the first story I could relate to. It was about a little boy named Pablo. Pablo had to help his father tend a small garden in the backyard, and he would go outside barefoot. The soil was so hot it burned his feet. Of course I could relate. I knew about going barefoot on a hot summer day and feeling the scorching ground under my bare feet.

My fourth-grade teacher, Ms. Laura Magnon, made me feel very special. She made me her teacher's pet and for that reason I wanted to please her. If learning the spelling words or the multiplication tables pleased her, then I would do it. She had come in to replace Mrs. Stahl, who had to leave early in the year. It was Ms. Magnon's first year teaching. Because of her, I realized school could be fun. I secretly wished she would adopt me. I imagined arriving to school with her and having my own room with my own bed that I did not have to share with my sisters. I dreamed she would teach me everything and I would be very smart. Ms. Magnon taught elementary school for only one year. After that year she left to teach science at a local high school. I did not realize it then, but she was my first role model. I thought of becoming a teacher like her. She retired after close to forty years of teaching, but before she did I told her that she had made fourth grade a great experience for me.

An early recollection from my childhood is hiding behind Norma, my oldest sister, as my grandmother, who lived with us, scolded me. I remember looking up at Norma and realizing she was protecting me, and ever since then I have looked up to her. Everybody needs a mentor, and mine is Norma. Years later I realized that consciously or unconsciously I was following in Norma's footsteps. For example, when she graduated from high school in 1965, I graduated from sixth grade. When she received her associate's degree in 1971, I received my high school diploma. Later, when she received her master's degree in 1976, I got my bachelor's. In 1982, Norma received her doctorate and I received a master's. For me, my academic achievements are but a journey with a road map that Norma has handed down to me. She has been there, helping me find my own path. We should all have someone to help us as we search for our life's path.

When I graduated from high school, I received a scholarship. Although I had applied for several scholarships, I did not expect to receive any, since my grades were not exactly stellar. I was an average student with good grades in mathematics. That scholarship of $150 was only enough for tuition for the first semester at Laredo Junior College. The second semester was funded partly by financial aid, partly by work-study, and partly by Norma. By working in the financial aid office as a work-study student, I learned how to apply for and obtain financial aid, which I received until I got my degree. My high school grades were fair, but when I started college my grades improved. I had become motivated to study and get better grades.

They Made a Difference...and That Has Made All the Difference

Parents are our first teachers. Mine certainly were. My father influenced me in a number of ways. I especially credit him with teaching me various applications of mathematics. He worked with Zachry Construction Company, so he did a lot of the carpentry work needed around the house. One summer my father enlarged our kitchen so it would better fit our growing family, and the project was a mathematical experience for me. Measuring angles using the *esquadra* (carpenter's square), a tool he used for calculating corners, and *la cinta de medir* (measuring tape) taught me about rulers and how to use them to measure in inches, feet, and yards, as well as in centimeters and meters. I remember feeling special when he allowed me to climb to the top of the roof with him and help him by passing the tools to him. On the roof it was just him and me. He showed me the ruler's markings and explained that half of one-half was one-fourth, pointing to the markings with his finger, deformed by severe arthritis. I much preferred learning math on the rooftop than being in the kitchen, learning math through recipes. I despised cooking and would do almost anything, short of ironing, to stay out of the kitchen… yes, even climb a roof, step on a rusted nail, get a tetanus shot, and have my mother tell me, "*Es lo que te sacas por no quedarte adentro.*" But I was not the *adentro* type. I wanted to be outside, where I could catch *camaleones* (lizards), climb trees, or be with Dad on the rooftop.

I am lucky to have had several mentors throughout my life: my oldest sister, Norma, Mrs. Judy Hunter, Dr. Cecilia Moreno, and Dr. Elvia Niebla. These women are true mentors and have, in their own way, influenced me and helped me get where I am today. Aside from my father's influence and my mother's support and help, I credit my sister with instilling in me a love of teaching. My sister Norma, ever since I can remember, has been there pulling, pushing, or doing a little bit of both, but never rushing me, always letting me decide for myself and allowing me to learn from my and her own mistakes.

As a teenager, Norma would set up a little *escuelita*, a small school for neighborhood kids in our backyard. She would gather all the neighborhood kids and teach them *canciones y cuentos*, along with the alphabet and nursery rhymes. I wanted to be a teacher like her. Later she taught at a local middle school, and I think that listening to her stories about the students inspired me to choose a career in teaching.

In high school I joined the Future Teachers of America (FTA). One of the activities of FTA that I greatly enjoyed was tutoring students at Leyendecker Elementary School once a week. For several summers, I also worked as a teacher's aide for the Head Start program and really enjoyed that. Mrs. Judy Hunter became a great role model during the last summer I worked for Head Start. Years later, I was a teacher of junior high school students, and Dr. Cecilia Moreno, the principal, always made me feel empowered. She encouraged me to pursue a PhD and offered to help me study for the GRE. When she asked professors from Texas A&M University at Kingsville to talk to a group of female teachers about graduate school, she invited me. I felt that she was genuinely interested in me and in advancing my education. Dr. Elvia Niebla is an inspiration as well. She inspires in me a belief that I am capable of accomplishing anything I want to. Dr. Niebla and Dr. Moreno's belief in me helped me decide to pursue a PhD.

It is important to have mentors and people who believe in you and support you. But it is equally important, if not more, to have a spouse who encourages you and is supportive of your career and education. Hilario and I met on Halloween night when I was seventeen and a junior in high school. He was a guest at my sister's wedding and asked me to dance a couple of dances that night. I was in high school and he was six years older. I must admit I thought he was too old for me. And anyway, I had a boyfriend serving in the army at the time, and I thought I would marry him when I finished school. But Hilario and I started going out, and we dated on and off for about five years before we got married. I quit college and stayed out of school for a year, and I thought that was the end of my college days. Fortunately, I was mistaken. Hilario encouraged me to go back to school and finish my degree. I eventually received my BS in elementary education in 1976. Soon after, I began teaching mathematics at my alma mater, L. J. Christen Junior High. I enrolled in a master's program and received my master of science in secondary education in 1982. By then I had two children, Klariza, my daughter, who was a little over two years old, and Nono, my son, who was then seven.

During all this time, I cannot think of a single instance when Hilario was not there to help with the kids. Countless times he made sure they were cared for. He would feed or bathe them, get them to school on time, or get them ready for bed. My children were taught at a very early age that if they needed a drink of water or got sick in the middle of the night, they were to call their dad. They learned to let me sleep because I often stayed up late grading papers, doing averages, or reading or writing for whatever course I was taking. Hilario not only helped with the kids and the house chores and encouraged me, he was also proud to tell people that I was working on my master's. Hilario has always been there for me, whether it was for work or for school. Sometimes he knows that I can handle a challenge even if I do not think I can. Getting an education is hard work that is made even harder by marriage; however, Hilario made it easier for me. I have heard stories of husbands getting upset because their wives had to study or do homework when they went back to college. In some cases, their anger has driven them to tear up books and completed homework. Unlike the husbands of these horror stories, Hilario understood that sometimes I had to study or read or use the dinner table as a desk for weeks or even months. He wanted me to study, to continue my education, and to graduate.

When I was accepted into the doctoral program (which he insisted I apply for because he knew I could do it), he was very excited for me. I believe much of what I have accomplished is due to his being such a supportive partner. He encourages me, believes in me, and helps me, but most important, he gives me the freedom I need to pursue my dreams.

Choosing a Path: *Pasos sin Veredas*

In her book, *Barefoot Heart,* Elva Treviño Hart, a computer analyst for IBM who became a writer and left behind a mathematics-oriented career, writes about her experiences with mathematics and why she initially chose that route instead of English. I, too, share Treviño Hart's sentiments in choosing a career in mathematics. During my junior high years, I developed a writing phobia. When I was in eighth grade, I was given writing assignments in my English class, and despite considerable effort, they were always returned for revisions; it seemed that I was not writing what the teacher wanted me to write. If only I could guess what the teacher wanted from me! However, I quickly realized that in math class, if I learned all the steps to a problem, the teacher would mark it correct. There was no guesswork involved. At that time students were taught that there was only one way to solve the problem, that the assignments were to be neatly done in pencil, and that the correct answer had to be legible and boxed in. If I executed all these steps accurately, I was certain I would get a good grade. That is why I began to like math. Like Treviño Hart, I had an inclination for writing and took pleasure in reading, but chose instead to follow a mathematical career.

Another reason I chose mathematics was my fascination with math riddles and tricks. I remember my father's riddles; one in particular always interested me. My father would start the riddle and I always tried to solve it. He would begin, "A bus driver"—with a name such as Don José or Paco—"was driving a bus with x number of passengers" (the number of passengers would always change). He would continue the riddle, "At each stop x number of passengers would get in, others would get off." I would try to keep up with the mental calculations of the number of people getting on and getting off at each corner. After several stops, my dad would ask, "Who is driving the bus?" It was a version of "As I was going to St. Ives, I met a man with seven wives." I always tried to figure out Dad's riddles. But this particular one I remember trying to figure out even days later. He was teaching me mental math and whetting my appetite for math-related games. However, I never thought I would be teaching mathematics one day.

I was certain, though, that I wanted to be a teacher. When the counselor at Laredo Junior College, now Laredo Community College, looked at my high school transcript and said, "I see that you have good grades in the math courses you've taken in high school—why don't you get your degree in education and become a math teacher," I readily agreed. Although earlier childhood experiences had steered me in the direction of math, it was not until I was asked what I wanted to major in that I finally realized it: I wanted to be a math teacher. When I started teaching, the more I taught, the more I liked it. I confess the first year was difficult, and several times I questioned my decision, but I am glad I persevered.

My college professors had taught me the theory behind how to teach, but that was not very practical as I faced my first class. My first teaching experience was with low-achieving, at-risk minority junior high students. On the first day, I walked in with a vision: I would ask my students to take out their books, follow my instructions, and be involved in learning as I explained the process. They would be fascinated with the beauty of mathematics, and I would make it come alive for them. Then they, with their papers and pencils in hand, would all do their assignments and complete their homework. I would teach and they would learn. Easier said than done! The reality I encountered shattered that vision. Teaching was not as easy as I thought it would be, especially because, as a new teacher, I was assigned to teach the at-risk students, many of whom came to school ill prepared and unmotivated to learn anything, much less mathematics. I had to find a way. Stimulating motivation was a big challenge with students who were faced with many obstacles: low reading ability, poverty, little or no parental involvement, gangs, drugs, and no drive to stay in school, much less perform well in school. While I knew that all students could learn if given the opportunity, I also knew that students must first want to learn. That was the catch. I had to instill in students the *ganas*, the desire and drive to want to learn for the sake of learning. I could not understand my students; they were so different from when I was in junior high. Unlike my students, I always wanted to go to school and not miss a single day. Even though my grades were not the best, I enjoyed school and I had the *ganas* to learn something new. They were not bad students, but they were students who had been left behind and were struggling to keep up, and many were frustrated with a system that worked against them. Years later, when I was searching for my research topic for my doctoral dissertation, I knew that it would have to deal with mathematics, but more specifically with student motivation to learn mathematics.

To never give up has been a tough lesson that I have learned. Countless times I was overwhelmed by the work that getting a PhD required and that my full-time job demanded. I became discouraged and felt that it was not for me–that I could not go on. But I knew this was a common feeling. I told myself what I have told others–they must believe in what they want to do and keep going until they achieve it. I tell my students that they have the capabilities to be successful in a career in science or mathematics, that those subjects are not any harder than others, and that they are just as capable of succeeding as anyone else. As my mother always told us, "*¿Si otros pueden hacerlo, porqué tú no?*" (If others are able to do it, why can't you?). We have to know that success depends on ourselves and that at times we set up our own obstacles. For example, I always doubt my ability to succeed or accomplish, and mentally discourage myself. Another piece of advice I have received, and have passed on, is to learn from my mistakes and not repeat the same mistake twice.

A common phrase that many teachers say, when asked what they do, is, "I am just a teacher." In fact, I have heard that statement from some of the best teachers I know. I used to think that way, too–I am just a teacher. But a teacher is never "just a teacher." A teacher has to be much more. I often wonder if a teacher is made or if a teacher is born to teach. Teaching is a hard job, but I know firsthand that teaching is the most important and rewarding job one can have. The most influential factor in a student's learning is the teacher. Research has shown that a significant positive correlation exists between good, effective teachers and students' high academic achievement.

It is sad to admit that some students go through their entire schooling and never have one special teacher. All it takes to make a difference is one good teacher at the right time. I always tried to be that good teacher. What pleasure I received from hearing students who struggled to understand a difficult concept exclaim, "Aha, I get it." I could almost see the lightbulb turn on. What a joy!

Over the course of my career, I have worked in many different positions. I served as the testing coordinator for the Laredo Independent School District, one of two districts in Laredo, Texas. The district had approximately twenty-three thousand students from prekindergarten to twelfth grade. I also served as an instructional coordinator (K–12), where I oversaw and coordinated the mathematics instruction for these grades. Before that, I was a mathematics classroom teacher for twenty-seven years, seventeen years in middle school and the other ten at the high school level, and I enjoyed those years a great deal. I am currently teaching preservice and inservice teachers how to teach in a "new" way, not necessarily the way they were taught. I want to encourage them to see the diversity of their student population, to notice the individual needs the student comes to school with, and to find ways to motivate each student individually by meeting their needs, for it is in the classroom that mathematicians and scientists are made, where young people begin to see themselves choosing such a path.

Overcoming Obstacles

I consider myself a shy person. I have a hard time talking in front of a group if they are not my students. I lose my voice, my throat hurts, I get red blotches around my neck, and I break out in a cold sweat. I have suffered from this condition for many years. I know that it is important for me to get over this problem, and I have tried everything I can think of. I have worn turtlenecks to hide the red blotches, I take deep breaths before addressing a group, and I do not look people in the eye. While I have learned to somewhat control or disguise the condition, this has been a great challenge and one of the biggest obstacles I have encountered. I believe this feeling may be due to some previous experiences or a lack of self-esteem. There have been times when I have felt inadequate or awkward. In my current position,

I am often asked to address groups, and I have noticed that the more I do these addresses, the more I can control my anxiety. So maybe there will be a time when I will not feel traumatized, and I can face a large crowd confidently and free of symptoms.

Fortunately, I have not experienced too many incidents of racism. However, when I spent a summer at the university to establish residency, I recall one incident that was awkward. I was enrolled in a mathematics course from the university's education department, and the syllabus called for a twenty- to thirty-page paper to be turned in and then presented orally to the rest of the class. The professor did advise us to write on our dissertation topics. Even though I read numerous articles and sources on my topic, and spent many afternoons and long nights researching, writing, and rewriting the paper, the writing phobia I had acquired in junior high made the writing difficult for me. Nevertheless, I turned the paper in the day it was due and waited for it to be returned. The day the professor returned the papers he handed back all but mine. He turned to me and said, "Can I see you outside?" When we were outside, he gave me my paper and said it was the best paper of all those from the class. I was so nervous by then that I took my paper, said thank you, and went back inside. As I think back now, I wonder why he did not say that to me while in class instead of going outside. Was he surprised, perhaps shocked, that a Latina from Laredo would be able to write a competent paper? In any case, the incident did not help build my confidence, and I still wonder what was behind his actions.

When I applied to the PhD program, I had no clue how to go about it. However, eventually the pieces all came into place. I knew I wanted to go for a PhD and had wanted to for a long, long time. I did not want to do it alone, so I asked, invited, suggested, and nearly begged several of my friends to apply with me. Only one did, though, and she enrolled in an EdD program in another institution and has since received the degree.

When I talked about my dream to get a PhD, people in general, but friends especially, were not particularly encouraging. I heard comments such as "You're too old for that" or "Are you crazy? You'll have to go away all summer and leave your husband and daughter." For example, my principal once told me, "The degree and twenty-five cents will get you nothing" and "What do you want that for? It's a lot of work for the thousand-dollar stipend the district will give you." I persevered and applied and was selected as one of a cohort of five educators to join five others who were two semesters ahead. I was set to start realizing my dream.

In the summer of 2000, I arrived at Texas A&M University to meet Dr. Charles Lamb, chair of my graduate committee. Early in our conversation he warned me that many people would ask why I wanted a PhD, and he posed the question himself. I started to answer, explaining the many things I could do with the degree—become a university professor and teach at that level, prepare preservice teachers, fulfill a dream, my goal, and… He stopped me mid-sentence and said, "That is not what I want to hear. The reason you are getting the degree is because you want to and you can. Period." Throughout my graduate work I kept his words in my mind and in my heart. "Because you want to and you can." Those few words have motivated me many times, especially when times get tough and I think I cannot achieve my dreams.

CHAPTER 9

A's for Academics, C's for Conduct

Diana Marinez
*Professor of Biochemistry
and Dean, College of
Science and Technology*

I was born and raised in Laredo, Texas, the oldest of three children. My brother is a year younger and my sister six years younger. I had a normal and, some might say, privileged middle-class upbringing, to some extent nontraditional for a girl growing up in south Texas in the 1940s and '50s. One of the things that was different is that both my parents worked. My father, Tomas R. Sánchez, was the manager of Sears, Roebuck and Co., and my mother, Consuelo "Chelo" Cuellar, was the credit manager for the Gateway Chevrolet Company. Both had worked up to these positions, as neither had a college degree. My family is related to the founders of Laredo, and we were considered a prominent family there, even though the money in my father's family had been lost by one of my grandfather's brothers. Consequently, my father, who intended to go to college and then to medical school, had to drop out during his junior year of college to help support the family. My mother went to secretarial school and started working before she got married, and, once married, continued working, which was not commonly done at that time. My father never seemed concerned that she worked outside the home.

Education was very important to my parents because they wanted their children to have what they had not been able to have. My early schooling was at Ursuline Academy, a private Catholic girls' school. I changed to the public school system in the eighth grade, when uniforms were introduced at Ursuline. I took one look at the uniform on me, and that was enough to say "Not for me." It was not that I was fashion conscious; I hated wearing dresses, actually, and my family did everything they could to entice me to be feminine. But I looked like a beanpole in the plaid uniform. Since my dad was the manager of Sears, he bought me a new dress weekly, which of course I promptly managed to ruin, either by tearing the hem out or by pulling off the ties of the bows at the waist (I did the latter because the nuns would use them to tie me to my desk quite often, even up to the seventh grade). At home and for play, I wore boys' shorts because they were cut more narrowly and fit my skinny body better. I also did not want long hair, because I hated having my hair braided every morning, so in the first grade I somehow persuaded my Aunt Yaya (Adelaida), my mother's oldest sister, to cut my hair. I ended up with a Buster Brown (or Prince Valiant, a popular comic strip) hairstyle, one that I kept up to high school.

I did well academically, and in elementary school was rewarded with quarters from my parents for my efforts. I loved the subjects of science and math the most. I also liked history, but I really did not enjoy writing or English class, as I had to work a lot harder at these subjects. I was an avid reader, using both the school and public libraries a lot. I read every Nancy Drew book published. But I did not take to grammar, spelling, or writing. While I would consider myself a smart person, I was by no means a "brain," even though many kids called me that. I was just willing to work hard because I wanted to do well.

I did not do well in the area of conduct, though. I finished my work quickly and then had nothing more to do, so I talked. The teachers did not keep me busy enough or have me do other things. The fact that I was a social type did not help. In spite of my conduct grades, my parents never scolded me, only asked me to try not to talk so much. I remember that my fourth-grade teacher, Ms. Zúñiga (yes, Martha Zúñiga's *tía*), had me sit next to her to keep me "under control," but she made the mistake of having my desk face the class. It was a perfect opportunity to perform. One day my antics got to her, and she walked me to the principal's office to begin proceedings to expel me. Somehow I managed to beg for forgiveness and promise to behave, and we returned to class. I must have improved, because I do not remember any other incident like this, at least not in the fourth grade. I do remember being tied to my desk in the seventh grade, though. My conduct grades never reached the A level until high school. I remember getting a C in conduct in the high school typing class, which a group of friends and I took in summer school. This grade kept my friend Angie and me out of the Courtesy Service Club our first year of high school. This was a highly desirable club that provided ushering for most school events. The girls each wore a white dress with a red sash and the letters CSC. To belong, you had to have good academic and conduct grades and be voted in. Both Angie and I were admitted the following year.

By the time I was in the fifth or sixth grade I had a BB gun. I did not get girl toys for Christmas; I asked for whatever my brother got. I got guns, trains, and of course a token doll every year, but it just sat there. I am sure my mother and my five aunts, all very proper ladies, hoped I would outgrow my tomboy tendencies when I hit puberty, but

Diana Marinez with her mother, brother Tom, and cousin Tony, 1946.

I have never really outgrown this behavior. With the BB gun I could shoot cans down at the creek, since I did not shoot at animals. But the first day I got the gun, I accidentally shot at and broke our neighbor's window, one that I had to replace (I did not receive an allowance). I must have had a streak of mischief in me or was dared, because I shot out the corner light several times. One time I even shot at some mean kids who were bothering us. I am not proud of this deviation of character, but as I was a "speck of a child," short and skinny to boot, I guess I compensated with a big mouth and an aggressive and fearless nature.

I might as well confess three other deviations of character that my family and friends still remember, and some feel should not be shared publicly. On one occasion I socked a guy in the chin who was picking on my brother, since my brother was not protecting himself. Fortunately, he was so shocked that a girl hit him that he did not hit me back. Another time, a neighbor, who was about five years older, teased me, so I picked up a rock, hurled it at him, and hit him in the head. He chased me around the house and never caught me. He ended up needing stitches from the blow. He never picked on me again, but this did not ruin the friendship. Then there was the time I got fed up with my brother, who was teasing me, as brothers tend to do, and I threw a butcher knife at him. Thank God I missed him. But do you think that stopped him? No! I must have pinched him black-and-blue, but apparently pain did not work on him. I have to admit that when I was young I had quite a temper, which I eventually learned to control.

In addition to going to school, I participated in the Girl Scouts, dancing lessons, music lessons, and whatever other learning opportunities arose, such as sewing and art. I remained a Girl Scout and took dance lessons until I graduated from high school. I actually learned to sew quite well at Singers, even though to this day I hate doing hems and putting in zippers. I enjoyed taking art classes in the summer, although an artist I was not, but I hated piano lessons, and my parents finally decided those lessons were a waste of money. I went to Girl Scout camp in Leakey, Texas, every year until I was in high school. I loved camping, though not necessarily the food, since I was a very picky eater, something I have outgrown. The first year I went to camp, when I was nine, there was a forest fire quite a distance away across the river that ran along the edge of the camp. All the girls in my group were crying for their parents except me. I thought it was exciting. I had the tendency to sleepwalk, so the counselors made sure my cot was surrounded by other cots. It is one thing to sleepwalk at home, but if you walked in the wrong direction from the tent at camp, you would end up over a cliff and in the river. Once I woke up while coming back from the outhouse, which I could not remember going to. Since I was not sure where I was, I started screaming for someone to come and help me return to the tent.

One summer our Girl Scout troop qualified to attend the National Roundup by attending Primitive Camp near Corpus Christi, where I was also chosen to represent the camp on a TV program in Corpus Christi. By high school my role at camp had changed from camper to counselor, and I have to admit it was payback time. I realized what a pain I must have been as a camper—a lovable pain, but a pain nonetheless. I was fortunate to have had dedicated women who took the time to provide us with experiences few girls get. I was especially close to Ms. Inky (Vera Enckhausen), the director of our council, and Ms. Young (Ruth Young), the PE teacher at Martin High School, who was active in the Girl Scouts. They took my energy and channeled it, keeping me busy and making sure I did not get into too much trouble for not following the rules and for being outspoken. To this day, I remain friends with many of the girls who were in my troop; we have been together since grammar school.

I also took ballet, tap, acrobatics, and Spanish lessons. I loved dancing. I was great at technique but not very graceful, so of course my favorite dance form was tap, which demanded less grace than drama. Even now I fantasize about being a ballerina or dancing to the great waltzes at a grand ball. One year, Rita Hayworth's parents, the Cansinos, taught Spanish dancing in Laredo. A single season of grueling practice convinced me that I did not want to dance professionally and that being a ballerina had to remain a fantasy. I regret now that I did not persist in playing piano, but the requirement of sitting for any length of time was not something I could manage as a child; anyway, my musical talent was in short supply. On top of that, my piano teacher was a neighbor who was big and scary to all the kids in the neighborhood. I was not particularly good at singing, either. I still cannot carry a tune. Although I joined the church choir and sang at many Masses, the choir director just tolerated me. My mother, on the other hand, loved to sing, and she sang well and often. She knew all the latest hits. She also played piano by ear, so we had a lot of music in the house. My aunts, especially Aunt Mary, took me to concerts and cultural events, too.

Career Choices

I do not believe there was any one person who was pivotal in my early life, who led me to choose a career in science. I always liked science, was good at it, and put a lot of time into the subject at school. This natural interest and ability was nurtured and supported in a variety of ways by a variety of individuals. We lived a block away from Chacon Creek in Laredo, and the lot across the street had no houses until I was in high school, so I considered the wooded lot (mesquite trees, of course) and the creek alongside our house to be our playground. When I was not reading, I was outside riding my bike, playing in the fort we had built, climbing mesquite trees, or roaming Chacon Creek. Our house faced Chacon Creek, and we could see the bridge on the highway to Zapata across the creek. You had to climb down a big cliff to get to the creek, which was dry unless it had rained. One of my favorite spots was a place we called the dripping cave, which was a cavelike formation on the side of the cliff facing the creek. The area had mica veins and was a great source for different rocks, which I of course brought home to add to my other rocks, collected on short trips to Mexico, mostly to Saltillo or Monterrey, where I spent time when I visited the Cola de Caballo and the Grutas de García, places similar to Carlsbad Caverns.

Since there was very little water in the creek, it was not a dangerous place with respect to water, but in other respects it could have been. Now that I am a mother, I cannot believe that nothing bad ever happened (such as getting bitten by a snake or the wild dogs that roamed the place, or running into strange men who were in the area). But my parents never forbade me from practically living there, barefooted, most of the days in the summer and after school. My feet became so tough I could even walk where there were a lot of *cadillos* (sticker burrs). My parents worked outside the home, and sometimes the maid who looked after us locked us out of the house so she could get her work done. Because my mother was to some extent a free spirit, and as the youngest in her family was allowed more freedom than her sisters had been, she allowed me those same freedoms. She knew I liked being outside and at the creek, and overall we lived in a safe place.

All of this reminiscing is to say that my childhood experiences shaped my very first career aspiration—geology. In high school, after taking biology and chemistry with two teachers I liked, I decided I would be a biochemist. There were no geology courses in the curriculum to further my interest in geology. My high school yearbook lists "Future Biochemist" under my picture. Did I know what this career was all about? Probably not. I thought it would be cool to do cancer research, and this was at least one thing I knew biochemists did.

Once I decided I would go into biochemistry, I never looked back or thought of anything else. I went about following all the steps necessary to accomplish my goal. I never thought I would end up in academia, much less in administration. I learned early the excitement of scientific discovery but also the amount of time and work it took. I also learned that I liked teaching and that I was good at it.

People in My Life

I have been fortunate to have a strong support system all my life. The list of those who supported my aspirations is long and, in retrospect, includes mostly women. After college, however, primarily men, and of course family and friends, influenced and supported me.

I was very fortunate that everyone around me, beginning with my parents, stressed education. My father made it clear I could do anything I wanted to do and be anything I wanted to be. This was not the message most young girls in Mexican American families along the border in south Texas during the 1940s and 50s received from their parents, relatives, and friends. My father never stifled my outspoken, "aggressive" tendencies (which would now be considered assertive), nor did he try to make me be a "proper young lady." He thought everything I did was "cute."

Oh, don't get me wrong; he was pretty strict and had a stern demeanor. My friends called him "Grumpy" for a reason, but they were not really afraid of him, just respectful. And even with his generally tolerant attitude, he did have some ideas that stood in contrast to his liberal ways. They seemed to surface more as I got older and went away to college. For example, when I was at Incarnate Word College (IWC), in San Antonio, I think he actually believed we were chaperoned when we went out, something that never happened when I was home and went out with "the boyfriend." When I asked permission to go to Houston to a dance with my steady, he said I could not go. Of course I went, because my mother knew my father could be unreasonable sometimes, and she told me I could go.

If it was inconvenient to have a strict father, it was also embarrassing. My junior year in college, I flew to Oak Ridge, Tennessee, to do undergraduate research. I failed to call home immediately when the plane landed, so Dad got the neighbor, who was connected to the governor, to send the state police out to Oak Ridge to find me. Can you imagine having the state police call the director of the National Labs to locate a twenty-one-year-old who had not called home? I thought I would die.

But overall, even with his apparent contradictory behavior that seemed to manifest itself most frequently later in life, my father in no way followed the norm for raising women at the time. My mother also supported everything I did, but her personality was different from my father's. She had a zest for life and an upbeat personality and always put on a happy face, even when she had one of her recurrent headaches. She had been a cheerleader while at Laredo High School, and she retained this peppiness, even in her walk, well into her eighties. This personality manifested itself even when she suffered from Alzheimer's, which eventually robbed her of most of who she was.

Though everything began with my immediate family, I have to add to them my aunts on both sides of the family. My mother's four sisters—Adelaida (Yaya), Ernestina (Tina), Otila (Tila), and María—were more traditional than my mother, and while they voiced their opinions and sometimes appeared judgmental, on the whole they did not impose their will, at least not on me. They not only supported whatever I was doing but also took me places: to visit Monterrey, to local music concerts, and to San Antonio for concerts and ballet. My father's sister, Ada Jo, was a real character—an independent and outspoken career woman who did not marry until later in life. She took my brother and me to San Antonio by train, where we stayed at the Menger Hotel and went to the zoo and rode elephants. She also gave me a job on Saturdays and in the summers at the Bon Ton, a women's specialty store she managed in Laredo. Of course, she paid me out of her own money, but I did not know that at the time. When she got married and moved to Odessa, I spent many summers there. She drove until she was into her eighties, but she was never able to pass the driver's license exam, so she drove without a license all her life. Also, she drove nonresident Mexican workers who worked for her and her friends in Odessa to Laredo, so they could journey back to Mexico. When she was eighty, she went with us to Colorado. We even camped in Mesa Verde and she slept in the van. She had angina and had no business being at high altitudes, and she could have easily died on this trip; as soon as she got back home, the doctor put her in the hospital and she underwent a quadruple bypass. When she recovered, she continued to "clog up the new bypasses," as my cousin put it, and continued to visit us in Michigan most summers.

When I had my own family, it was not unheard of for us to travel with my mother, as well as with one or two aunts (usually Otila and Ada) or cousins, or my mother-in-law or sisters-in-law. In fact, I can barely remember a trip taken with only my nuclear family. I have to hand it to my husband, who actually encouraged this large entourage. Imagine a trip to Philadelphia and Washington DC, planned around the pickup of daughter Danielle from gymnastics camp in Pennsylvania, which included Juan and me; Carola, our oldest daughter; my mother, Chelo; Aunt Otila; my cousin Otila; Otila's nieces, Adriana and Laura; my Aunt Ada; and my mother-in-law, Frances—ten women and one man in all. The only aunt who never traveled with us was my Aunt Yaya (Adelaida). I called her *"la coronela,"* the colonel. She was a homebody who, after her husband of three years was killed, took care of the house for her married sister, Tina, and her unmarried sister, María. Rose in *The Golden Girls* (played by Betty White)—that is my Aunt Mary. I learned to drive in Aunt Mary's car, a 1947 Chevy with ten thousand miles on it; it became my first car in 1957. It was a shock to the car to be driven over thirty miles an hour by a fourteen-year-old. Yes, I had my license when I was fourteen, so this means I was driving when I was thirteen. I had to look between the wheel and the dashboard to see out the window. I have no idea how I reached the clutch, because I was just under five feet tall.

My Aunt Tina worked at what was then City Drug in downtown Laredo, which was next to the Plaza Theater, a half block away from the Tivoli Theater and a block from Sears, so I saw her when I was at the movies or visiting my father at the store. I thought it was cool that I could go to the soda fountain and charge whatever I wanted to drink or eat. Aunt Tina appeared in *Ripley's Believe It or Not* because she had worn flowers in her hair for heaven only knows how many years. She and my Uncle Armando often took me to Monterrey. In those days, the cars did not have air conditioners, so I always asked my uncle to drive faster. He told me that fast speeds were not good for the tires. I did not believe him, as he was a rather pokey driver anyway.

My grandmother, Ida Herf Dodd, or Mamayita, lived with us when we were young, and from her I acquired my love of cooking. She let me help her in the kitchen when I was a very young child, and she took me to the grocery story, the Piggly Wiggly. When my grandparents moved out of our house, I still spent a lot of time with them, as they lived close to Martin High School.

As mentioned previously, Ms. Vera Enckhausen, director of the Girl Scouts, Ms. Ruth Young, our high school PE teacher, who was heavily involved in girl scouting, and many Girl Scout troop leaders provided a venue for exploring the outdoors and enjoying the camaraderie of women. I learned many skills and the importance of involvement, and from these experiences I realized the importance of working with youth and the difference this can make in a person's life.

From my dancing teacher, Ruby Roy Galo, I learned commitment, perseverance, posture (stand tall and straight), coordination, and to never say "I can't" but rather "I'll try." I attended dance class every afternoon after school until about six o'clock. Ms. Galo inspired us to work hard and taught us how to improve or master what we were learning. She worked us hard, but she was not a strict disciplinarian.

My high school biology teacher, Elia Montemayor, and especially my chemistry teacher, Ellen deTournillon, continued to ignite my interest in science and provided an excellent foundation for college. To this day, I remain friends with my high school chemistry teacher and her family, and it is amazing to me how many students from Martin High School she inspired to continue in chemistry. As she was a graduate of IWC, this is the college I chose for my undergraduate work. We reconnected after high school, when I was a postdoc at the Institute of Marine Science at the University of Miami. I knew her family had moved to Miami, so I called Ellen when I arrived. I practically lived at their house, since it was like being with family. Since then, we have kept in touch, and she has continued to be a friend and mentor. In fact, she has traveled most years to the reunions of Martin High School's '50s graduates, so it is not just me but a generation of students she has touched, many of whom she turned into chemists. Teachers do make a difference!

Sister Mary Daniel Healy, my chemistry professor at IWC (now University of the Incarnate Word), took me under her wing, told me I was heading to graduate school, and provided me with the education and experiences I needed, including the developing of personal character. She was interested not just in her students' intellectual development but also in the development of the whole person. She was as demanding about our personal appearance and behavior as she was about our academic growth. From my experiences at IWC, I learned that educational programs needed to be student focused and include more than just courses. I have found that women who have been educated at women's colleges and Catholic colleges seem to have gotten this same message. I believe this is why I was an effective chair at Michigan State University and dean at Texas A&M University–Corpus Christi. Sister Mary Daniel taught me the importance of putting students first, rather than yourself or your university, and that if you did this, good things for yourself and the university would follow. This is why I made sure I spoke with all our students and parents during orientation days. I wanted to set the tone. For the parents, I talked about the college programs, but, more important, I talked about how they could help their child be successful and about "letting go," something that Latino parents find especially hard to do. Students got the "loving mother from

Diana Marinez as an undergraduate researcher at Oak Ridge National Laboratory, 1962.

hell" talk, in which I spoke frankly about what it takes to succeed. Sister Mary Daniel was there for me, and she taught me the importance of being there for students and being frank with them. She remains a good friend, and our second daughter, Danielle, is named after her.

By the time I was in graduate school, my mentors became primarily men because there were so few women faculty members. In graduate school, I chose to work with a professor in the microbiology department, Dr. Bill Finnerty, rather than someone in the biochemistry department, and in so doing was protected from either department's politics. Dr. Finnerty ran his lab professionally but also like a large family, so it was a very comfortable and supportive environment.

My second postdoc mentor is especially memorable too, and working for him led me into academia and also marriage. Somehow, Dr. Robert Cook convinced me to return to the cold Midwest, to Michigan State University, from a postdoc in marine science at the Institute of Marine Science. He convinced me that the Big Ten was the place to be. I went from working on enzymes in micro-organisms in graduate school to working on enzymes in the tentacles of the Portuguese man-of-war in Miami, then to enzymes in cow mammary gland tissue in the dairy science department at Michigan State University. I was the first postdoc in the department and a Hispanic woman to boot. Talk about culture shock for both of us—the department as a whole and me. Nevertheless, I grew professionally and personally, and ended up with a faculty position at Michigan State University, which I kept for twenty-five years. I met my husband there while he was still an undergraduate. The Cooks are Danielle's godparents even though they are not Catholic, a minor detail I failed to mention to the priest; since Sister Mary Daniel is also her godmother, I thought that God would forgive this little detail. The Cooks remain good friends, and we are as much a part of their family as they are of ours.

It may sound strange, but I consider the Society for the Advancement of Chicanos and Native Americans in Science (SACNAS) as a whole, and some specific individuals whom I met through SACNAS, to have been instrumental in the development of my career. Drs. Joe V. Martínez, Bernardo Ortiz de Montellano, Elma González, and María Elena Zavala have been not only friends but also mentors, as well as partners in making a difference for Latinos and Latinas in science. They keep me honest.

My husband certainly did not follow the traditional role of the eldest in a large Mexican American family with respect to his wife and children. We both had to learn to negotiate how we would best nurture family as well as career. In fact, it was only through Juan's urging that I applied for the dean position at Texas A&M University–Corpus Christi, and without his support and commitment to giving back to our south Texas community, my career away from home would have never worked, much less flourished. My in-laws, Frances and Efraín Marinez, were there every step of the way, and I have often joked with Juan that if he wanted to move, he would have to move his mother with us. Our daughters have never really complained about my time away from home or about my community work, probably because I was already involved in those things by the time they were born, and they did not know any other life. Our eldest daughter, though, still says that I left home when I left Michigan and moved to south Texas; while they were supportive, it did come at a cost.

I would be remiss if I did not mention my sister and all my girl-friends, childhood friends who have always been there for me. They keep and have kept me sane, and they have worked with me to provide opportunities for other women and Latinos. Two of my closest friends are now deceased, but their influence continues.

Obstacles and Challenges

Identifying and discussing obstacles does not come easy to me, because while I am not naive, I have always chosen to look at obstacles as challenges that I needed to deal with in one way or another to get the job done. The obstacles had to be taken into consideration when developing a strategy. If I could not work through them, I would go over them or around them or simply wait them out. I figured I was smart and could eventually overcome them. I have always been a risk taker, but I always take calculated risks. I do like to win and be successful. But there are a few obstacles, or challenges, that I do still remember.

In high school I can remember only two instances when some-one tried to discourage my interest in pursuing a career in science. A Mexican medical doctor who was interning in the United States, a friend of my fathers's, told me that medical school was too difficult and not the best place for women. I told my father's friend that I did not have any desire to go into medicine anyway, and that if I ever did I could deal with it. My counselor in high school told me I did not have the talent to go into the sciences. I already knew that going into science was not something that very many women did, and her advice did not carry any weight with me, because my grades were certainly good enough. I have always wondered, though, what her basis was for these thoughts that she then shared with me. I also wonder how many other students have been discouraged by her and other counselors. Unfortunately, even today I can cite several examples in which counselors in south Texas have been less than supportive of young Latino males and females aspiring to go into the sciences and preprofessional fields. And we are in the twenty-first century! My awareness of such barriers, then, goes all the way back to high school, because previous to that I had not really run into any barriers other than the social ones I was very well aware of growing up in south Texas.

Professionally, the first major challenge came when I was a postdoc in the dairy science department at Michigan State University. Every year, the department had an annual conference, which included a fishing trip in northern Michigan. I was informed that women were not allowed to attend, even though all the men who helped in the barn could go. I first tried to address this issue internally, since I had the full support of my mentor, but I was told that the faculty wives did not want women to attend, and that even if I filed a grievance, it would not help. I filed a grievance nonetheless, and they ended up having to allow women. My boss was not the most popular person in the department after that, but he remained very supportive of his female students and staff. To date, everyone who worked for him is still in contact with him, and we periodically get together. Prior to then, I had not experienced such overt sexism, and while I had always been an advocate for women, this incident solidified my commitment and converted me into a more proactive advocate.

When I started teaching and became pregnant in the early 1970s, I requested a leave of absence. I mention this action not because it was an obstacle, but because at that time Michigan State University did not have a policy for faculty who became pregnant. It could have become an issue, but when the leave was not approved, the chair of the Department of Natural Science claimed I was doing a project for him. I understood that when a university is on the quarter system, it is difficult for the students to adjust to a new teacher after six weeks of a ten-week term. I also felt, however, that with the increase of women faculty of childbearing age, major changes needed to be made in the benefits provided to women faculty. While I do not consider myself a pioneer, I was one. How I work with women faculty and dual-career couples certainly has been influenced by this experience.

The greatest challenge I faced during my twenty-five years at Michigan State University was presiding over the dissolution of the Department of Natural Science, a large interdisciplinary general education teaching department. In 1984, I became chair of this large and demoralized department, although I had never aspired to be an administrator. In fact, as a young faculty member I was often anti-administration; the last thing I wanted to be was an administrator. But some colleagues convinced me I should apply, as it was an internal search and they knew I was a strong advocate for faculty and students. I applied, and ended up with the full support of the faculty. The dean who appointed me indicated that now I was going to receive some of what I had been "dishing out" to administrators on campus. As it turns out, not only did I like administration, but I was good at it. As a chair, I was in the information flow loop, which gave me a more complete picture of the educational process than I had received as a faculty member. Information is power, and having access to it made me a more effective advocate for faculty and students. In five years, I was able to turn a demoralized and dying department into a vibrant and productive one. Unfortunately, these results did not protect us from the politics of the discipline departments, not having sufficient student credit hours and needing the credit hours that we generated by teaching all the required science courses for nonscience majors. The decision was made to dissolve the department in 1989, assign most of the faculty to their discipline departments, and create the Center for Integrative Studies within the college, in which faculty from the disciplines would teach "real science" to the freshmen. The transitional year was stressful because faculty were unsure of the department they would be in, and because of the devaluing of our intellectual mission as a general education department. Our colleagues in the discipline departments did not make the transition any easier, although all but a few of our faculty members were accepted to most departments. I learned that there are humane ways of implementing mandated decisions, no matter how difficult the changes may be.

I went to the biochemistry department in 1989, a department that was not too happy to have me. Their view was that I should move to the College of Education, since I was interested in education, especially the education of nonscience students. I had spoken with the College of Education, and their view was that I did not have the education course background necessary to make a contribution to their college. While this career experience was not positive, I learned how far apart scientists and educators are with respect to science and math education, and the barriers both have to overcome to provide effective education. I also had to find other avenues in order to continue the work I was doing. I became the education program director at the Julian Samora Research Institute, which had recently been formed. With this program, I had the opportunity to work on a community-based educational reform program we had designed, and was able to make some real differences in the greater Lansing Latino community.

Then, in 1994, I applied for and was selected to be the dean of the College of Science and Technology at Texas A&M University–Corpus

Christi. Even though I had had a very successful five years as a chair of a department, I had never aspired to be a dean, though I did miss administration and being in the middle of the action. I again had to be convinced to apply, but once I made up my mind, I aggressively sought the position. I was interested in the position because it was at a Hispanic-serving institution, because it would give me the opportunity to return to south Texas, and because I would be giving back to our community. I would also have the opportunity to help build a college–a very rare opportunity–and make a difference in providing quality math and science education to south Texans. I also felt that the institution needed someone like me, but I can assure you that it was only because the provost was a Latino that I was offered the position. Accepting the position meant being away from my family; had my husband and I not shared the same commitment to giving back to our community, being separated for twelve years would have never worked. Again, as when I had been chair, the faculty and I built a vibrant college in ten short years, and we made a difference in science and math education.

Had I the chance to do it over, would I go into the sciences again? Yes. Would I recommend young women with an aptitude and interest in science to go into science? Very definitely. Today, there are fewer barriers and greater support systems, even though it is less than an even playing field. It is best to have a plan and be focused, but open to opportunities that arise. We often limit ourselves by not finding out if, in fact, we really do not like something. I would never have pictured myself as an administrator, but I took the risk and took that road, and I have flourished.

CHAPTER 10

On the Inside, Looking In

The Roots of a Life in Science

Lydia Villa-Komaroff
Chief Executive Officer
and Chief Scientific Officer

*T*here was never any doubt that my five siblings and I would go to college, or that my sisters and I, as well as my three brothers, would be professionals. The roots of this idea came from both sides of the family. My maternal grandfather, Manuel Larrañaga, had his daughters educated because he did not want them to marry cowboys. His sons, who would run a ranch, needed only enough education to sign their names and check the sums they received for cattle. My maternal grandmother, Margaret, as well as my great-aunt Erslinda, taught in one-room schoolhouses in different places in New Mexico after they graduated from Normal School in Las Vegas, New Mexico. They each lived alone in a small house provided by the community and would ride their horses to visit each other on weekends. From their stories of this time, I learned how satisfying independence could be.

My grandmother married but later divorced her husband, leaving everything behind, except her three children, when she left him.

Grandma Margaret raised three children as a single working mother, and so I learned that a woman could care for herself and her loved ones by her own efforts. After her stint as a teacher, she sold chemical toilets to farmers and ranchers in New Mexico and Arizona, and then became one of the first social workers in New Mexico. I believe that my mother went to college in part because Grandma felt that she did not get the promotions she deserved because she did not have a college degree. My great-aunt Erslinda, whom we called Aunt Linda, married Gregorio Chávez, a man who loved rocks. He adored her, and indulged her as her father had. She became famous as a demanding and loving teacher. When I visited her, people would stop us in church, in the stores, and even at the U.S. Immigrations checkpoint outside the city, to pay their respects and thank her. Aunt Linda and Uncle Greg never had children, and so I learned that women need not be mothers to be happy and fulfilled. Aunt Linda told me that my great-great-grandfather, Dr. Cristobal Larrañaga, saved thousands of children in New Mexico from smallpox by using a troop of orphaned boys as carriers of a vaccine. He infected two boys with cowpox, a mild disease that creates immunity to smallpox. As they traveled from town to town, liquid from the cowpox pustules was used for the vaccinations and to infect two more boys, who produced more vaccine. This story was later verified in part in *Albuquerque, Feliz Cumpleaños: Three Centuries to Remember*, a book by Nasario García.

My mother, Drucilla, was the middle child; she had an older sister, Melita, and a younger brother, Elfego. She was the first to go to college. She always worked, even with six children at home, and the few times she was between jobs, she was clearly not as happy. And so I learned that a woman could find work fulfilling and important.

My paternal grandfather left Mexico during the Mexican Revolution. He was a legal immigrant only because the laws that would make him illegal had not yet been written. His wife, Luz, was a *curandera*, a healer, who knew how to set a leg and cure various ailments with herbs. She was also diabetic and died at a relatively young age because she lived before insulin was available. My father, John, was a middle child in a family of nine boys and two girls. His mother, for reasons lost in memory, designated him the one to be educated. My older uncles left school after three or four years and went to work. But my dad and, later, his younger brothers were expected to finish high school. Dad, like his brothers, learned to play guitar and violin by ear, and by the time he was thirteen, he was earning money by playing in the street. A music teacher heard him, and taught him how to read music and hold the violin correctly. He enlisted in the air force and became a tail gunner when World War II broke out. Once, his gun jammed, and he took off his glove to fix it. His fingers froze to the metal and he tore the skin off as he frantically worked to unjam the gun. Ever after, he could not play the violin unless he wore tape on the fingers of his left hand. In England, he heard Yehudi Menuhin and Jascha Heifetz, and decided that he wanted to be a violinist like them, so he entered college on the GI Bill. He later said that he probably would not have gone to college if he had known that it was already too late for him to become a concert violinist.

My parents met after the war and were married three months later. I was born nine months after that. Over the next ten years, I was joined by three brothers, Richard, Roland, and Lorenz, and two sisters, Kathryn and Dorthea. My parents were opposites in many ways. Dad was a Roman Catholic, as many, probably most, Mexican Americans were. He was darkly handsome, with his Mexican Indian heritage written in his features. Mother was a Baptist and very fair, with blue-green eyes and auburn hair revealing her Basque heritage. My father believed that rules and laws, except his, were advisory rather than compulsory. He was a charismatic man and very persuasive. We were often short on money despite the fact that both Mom and Dad worked. He once used a car as collateral for loans from two different banks despite the fact that the car had no engine and was on concrete blocks in our backyard. He was a regular at pawnshops around the city, finding treasures such as a gold-trimmed set of *The World's Greatest Literature* or a guitar with no strings. Sometimes he would sell the items he found; sometimes he would hock them for a brief time to get cash necessary for bills or food. Despite his rather casual attitude toward laws, he had strong principles and a strong sense of right and wrong. I learned that one had a responsibility to examine and question official authority; defiance and disobedience were acceptable, but one had to act with the willingness to accept the consequences of such actions.

He was a music teacher in the Santa Fe school system. He had a disagreement with the administration, and he was moved to non-music classes in junior high and then grade school. At one point, he left the school system to sell insurance, but he returned to the schools after a year. I viewed my father as a heroic Robin Hood figure, and did not understand Mother's strength and determination until I left home. While Dad brought home books, it was Mother who read them to us. My mother read us stories aloud, and soon I was reading with her. I have no memory of learning to read, only that at some point the shapes on the page did not need her voice to have meaning. She was a social worker for many years and would not get home until after five o'clock. When I was in the second grade, I was in a school performance, and she made me a wonderful fairy costume with wings of white frosted paper and gauze. I felt utterly enchanting in it and wore the costume until it was grey and tattered. Mom loved to garden, and the front yard, at least, was always a colorful riot of flowers.

Mother had rheumatic fever as a child and had missed most of a year of school. As a result, she was never comfortable with arithmetic or math. She said the year she was out of school was when fractions were explained. We knew that she had been an honor student despite her math problems, and she remained one even after skipping a grade. Instead of repeating the year, she was simply put in the next grade when she got back to school, and she remained a top student. When I was thirteen and my youngest sister was three, my mother went off to school in Louisiana to get a master's degree. One of the required courses was statistics. Although she said she was terrified of the course, it was also apparent that she was working very hard at it. She sought help from her classmates and professors and passed the course. She proudly said, "And not with the lowest passing score, either!" What a perfect way to teach us that not being good at or comfortable with a subject was no excuse for not doing well in it.

While she was in school, Dad would call her every night and sing a love song to her. Our parents were a couple whose love for each

Lydia Villa-Komaroff with her family, 1963.

other was evident most of the time. They had their rough spots, and those times were evident, too. It was particularly unusual that in the macho culture in which we grew up, my father respected my mother's ambitions. It was a marriage of equals.

Languages and Secrets

Although my memories of childhood are happy and chaotic, they are also colored by a sense of secrecy and by mysteries. My parents had been punished for speaking Spanish in the schoolyard as they were growing up. Thus, they made a decision that we would be raised with English as our only language. Spanish became the language that the grown-ups used to discuss secrets. It was years before I learned that my maternal grandfather was not dead, that Grandma Margaret had left him because of his drinking. He followed her and took my mother, then age five, back to Denver with him. I never learned how long she was separated from Grandma, how Grandma got her back, or what Mother thought about this experience. I suspect it underlay both my mother's vulnerability and her strength. My grandfather appeared in our lives about the time I was ten. Grandma's face was uncharacteristically flushed, and she sparkled in a way I had not seen before. He asked her to rejoin him as his wife and she refused, but she was glad to have been asked and did not appear to regret her choices. Grandpa visited with us twice. He had diabetes and a jolly roguish look, even though one leg had been amputated. In my teens, I began to hear allusions to Mother's half family, another set of relatives in Denver. I never met them, but Mom went to see them and visited her father at least twice before he died.

My paternal grandfather, Encarnación Villa, died when I was about five, and the strongest memory I have of him is a vision of him standing in the road, a gray cowboy hat on his head, watching us drive away after a family visit. I watched him shrink in the distance until he was no longer visible. This is a sad and vivid memory, and I don't know why—another mystery.

Visits to my father's family were confusing and very mysterious to me. Since I knew so little Spanish, I did not understand the conversation and drew conclusions from the interplay of emotions and reactions across the faces of the grown-ups. There was always music in Grandfather's house; everyone played guitar or violin or mandolin. My uncles would sing Mexican folk tunes that were sad, or wildly romantic, or both. There was laughter and music, and beer or whiskey, and an explosive undercurrent. When I was older, I learned that my grandfather and some of my uncles were alcoholics. As a child I never saw my father drunk, but at some level I suppose I must have thought it a possibility.

Because I did not speak the language of my heritage, I felt I was different, and even though I was part of this large, loving, extended, vibrant family, I felt, in an important way, not part of it. I was on the inside, but I still felt I was looking in. This feeling was therefore very familiar when I entered the scientific world. By the time I took my first job, I had a pedigree that was as good as it could be. I had trained with the best scientists in the world, and had worked side by side with giants. I was as much a part of the scientific elite as any starting assistant professor, but I often did not feel that I fully belonged. However, I had learned that what counted was not so much how I felt, but how I acted.

School and the Path to Science

I was a good student, graduated eighth in my high school class, and was a Merit Scholar finalist. Not only did my parents have high expectations of me, but I was fortunate to be in a school where my academic prowess was rewarded. Many of my teachers were Mexican Americans or Hispana/os (*Latino* was not used in New Mexico). In grade school, there was a program called "Readers Are Leaders," part of which was a contest to see who could read and report on the most books each month. In junior high, our principal, Mr. López, made it possible to earn a school letter for scholastics as well as for athletics. These kinds of programs reinforced my parents' high expectations. Nevertheless, only 10 percent of my high school graduating class went to college, and there was a very high dropout rate, especially among Mexican American students.

The encouragement of my immediate family was very important, as there were members of my large extended family who did not value education or learning as highly as my parents did. Some of my cousins would not ask about grades but simply say, "Did you pass?" I also remember one aunt exclaiming, when she caught me reading a *Reader's Digest* condensed book, "How can your mother let you read that, there will be nothing left for you to read when you grow up!" I was in the fourth or fifth grade at the time, and for several weeks I rationed my reading, terrified at the thought of running out of reading material. Not reading was such unusual behavior for me that someone finally noticed and reassured me that I would never run out of things to read.

As a child I was a tomboy and, when not in school, was either riding a bike or reading. Through reading I both explored the world and escaped from it. I imagined myself as an explorer, a pirate, a cowboy— in my imagination I was almost always a boy, since they seemed to have the most satisfying roles. The strong women in my life made it possible for me to consider roles that were traditionally for men without feeling inadequate for being female. My father reinforced my sense that I could do anything that I wanted to do.

By the time I was nine, I knew that I wanted to be a scientist, even though I wasn't entirely sure what a scientist did. My image of a scientist came from a jumbled composite of science fiction stories, a longing for a retreat of my own, a desire to find answers. I think I had come to the conclusion that a scientist was an explorer and that while there were not many women scientists, there were some, and so I could be a scientific explorer even if there were other kinds of exploration that were closed to me because I was female. Since I had an uncle who had a master's degree and was a chemist, I also knew people like me could be scientists. Uncle Ishmael showed me a paper he had written for the *Journal of Organic Chemistry*, "Nitration and Bromination of m-Phenoxyanisole," and he said it was easier to write than a book report. That impressed me!

When I was deciding about college, I did not consider schools in New Mexico, where I grew up. I could not articulate it at the time, but

Lydia Villa-Komaroff, the only girl in her high school physics class, 1965.

I felt that if I went to college in New Mexico, I would never leave the state. I applied to the University of Washington because my father's brother and his family lived there, and I did not apply to any other college. I was accepted, and one summer day I got a postcard letting me know that tuition would increase by twenty-five dollars. I was already very worried about money. I had a small scholarship from our church, and although I had worked as a waitress, I had not saved much money; most of the money had gone to household expenses. My dad was mowing the lawn as I told him of the increase, and I said that maybe I should reconsider and apply to the University of New Mexico, as they had offered me a full scholarship. He stopped, wiped his brow, and said, "*Hija*, how much money do you have now to go to college?" "You know," I replied a little resentfully, "none." "Well, then," he said, "how much difference is twenty-five dollars going to make?"

One of my junior high teachers, Laura Beheler, remained a friend as we both moved on to high school. She taught English and physical education to ninth graders and was equally demanding on the soccer field and in the classroom. She encouraged competition and praised hard work. When I was ready to go to college, she called me and took me to meet a friend of hers. I left that house with a check for three hundred dollars, enough to pay my tuition deposit and at least start the school year. I got on a Greyhound bus and slept all the way to Seattle.

I enrolled as a chemistry major, because I wanted to be a physiologist like Hans Selye, the great physiologist who described the human stress response. I first read about Hans Selye in a *Reader's Digest* article when I was a junior in high school. The article described his work on elucidating the stress response in humans and rats. This was the first time I realized that a person could find an explanation for something by doing experiments. I knew one could do an experiment to see what happened, but the idea that something could be observed in the world and then explained by doing experiments was an astonishing revelation. I decided that I would find out how to be the kind of scientist that Selye was. The summer between my junior and senior years, I attended a National Science Foundation Summer Science Training Program at Texas College in Tyler, Texas. I spent several weeks doing lab work and library research, and found a group of people that liked science as much as I did. In this group, it was okay to be a "brain." Since there were as many girls as boys, and more people of color than whites, I also got the strong message that science was inclusive. The program allowed me to buy *Calciphiaxis*, a textbook by Selye that was not available in the college library. I was also allowed to purchase several white rats to study the effects of adrenalectomy. I don't recall the experiments. I do remember the excitement of planning experiments, the late-night discussions, the deep satisfaction after a day in the lab. I also began to realize how challenging it was to plan experiments that gave meaningful results, how very satisfying it was to decipher a little meaning from turgid text. I returned home to New Mexico with the surviving rats and a determination to become an endocrinologist, the same kind of physiologist as Selye.

Before I left New Mexico for college, I wrote to George Martin at the University of Washington, asking what I should do as an undergraduate to become an endocrinologist. Dr. Martin replied that I should major in chemistry, which is why I began my undergraduate career as a chemistry major. I was also accepted into the honors program. When I got to the University of Washington, I expected every class to be interesting and every professor to be scintillating. My grades plummeted as I discovered the allure of a social life and confronted for the first time the necessity of imposing discipline on myself. My college grades were checkered the first three years. My grades in math classes never got above a C, and I struggled to get a B in the introductory chemistry classes.

When I got a D in quantitative analysis, I went to see my advisor for the first time. He responded by saying, "Of course you're having trouble, women don't belong in chemistry!" I did not question this response, and I changed my major to zoology. I found zoology a boring collection of facts to be memorized, with none of the excitement I had felt in Texas. I briefly considered a major in history and was equally unexcited by the large lecture class that was required. Dr. Selye's books had led me to read about Claude Bernard, the French physiologist who defined homeostasis. I thought that perhaps I could combine my interest in science with history, and took a class in the Department of Biomedical History with Dr. Charles Bodemer, the department chair. Here, I once again found the excitement of discovery, now in the library instead of in the lab. In the meantime, I failed organic chemistry but got an A in the organic chemistry lab. I began to realize that if I wanted to go to graduate school, I'd better start paying more attention to grades. So I retook organic chemistry and made an A. I also began to take classes in the newly formed biology major. These classes, in animal behavior and developmental biology, were exciting and demanding. I was back on track.

The developmental biology class taught by Robert Cahn was particularly exciting. In retrospect, I am amazed at the resources devoted to this class for undergraduates. We learned how to reveal a developing chick embryo so we could compare the development of the living embryo with slides of different stages of chick embryo development. We used radioactivity and research drugs to see the effect of stopping protein synthesis or RNA synthesis on our developing chick embryos. We camped in the lab and set up shifts so that we could look at developing frog eggs every hour for seventy-two hours, and describe the processes of blastulation and gastrulation as revealed by flash-freezing embryos and sectioning them with razor blades. We read scientific papers, and sometimes one of the authors would visit and describe their work. One I particularly remember was John Gurdon, whose work was described in our textbook and whose papers we had pored over and struggled to understand. I had expected a sober old man and was struck by his youth, enthusiasm, and very red hair.

In the meantime, I worked in the medical school library as a work-study student, and one evening while I was on my break, a medical student tripped me in the cafeteria. It was, apparently, the only way he could figure out how to meet me. I was appropriately annoyed and promptly dismissed him as just another jerky medical student. However, the next day he came up and offered to take me to the local Viennese pastry shop as penance for his actions the day before. As a poor undergraduate, an offer of expensive pastries was irresistible. We talked for hours that night. The medical student, Tony Komaroff, was a senior in medical school, and I was a sophomore. His room-mates accused him of robbing the cradle, and we fell in love. Tony's entry into my life added a new element to my deliberations about my grades and future. He was a highly successful medical student, look-ing forward to an internship in New York or Boston. I began to think that this was someone I might consider a future with. Once again, I made an important choice that I could articulate only years later. I fell in love with a man who did not share my heritage, but who shared some of the best features of the men in my family—he was very smart and funny, he took it for granted that I was planning a career, he loved music. On the other hand, he lacked that indescribable feature we call machismo, which I associated with repressed violence. He was strong without swagger, and loving without possessiveness.

After Tony's graduation and at the end of my sophomore year, we packed all our possessions into Tony's VW Bug and drove to LA, where I met Tony's mother, Jackie, who was small and blonde and very welcoming. We then drove to New Mexico in the blue Mustang that Jackie gave Tony as a graduation present, and Tony met my large, rambunctious family. Our plan was to drive to New York, where we'd spend a few days before Tony began his internship in Boston. I'd then return home to work my summer job. The day we left for New York, my father gruffly called us into the living room. Without explanation, he asked us to kneel, then he put one hand on each of our heads and blessed us.

As I completed my junior year in Seattle, I began to look into transferring to the East Coast. While we had made no long-term commitment, it was clear that one of us would have to move to give our relationship the chance to develop to the point where we could decide if a long-term commitment was feasible. After his internship, Tony was fortunate to get into a program in Bethesda, Maryland, with the Regional Medical Program of the Public Health Service instead of being drafted for Vietnam. Robert Cahn, a professor who took an interest in me, recommended that I consider Johns Hopkins as a place where I could continue in biology and also continue biomedical history. Hopkins took only men in the undergraduate program, so Bob introduced me by letter to Gairdner Moment, a professor at Goucher College, a small women's college in Towson, Maryland.

I wrote to the admissions office at Goucher and received a rather chilly response—no room in the dorms, rather late for financial aid. Fortunately, in the next day or two, I also received a letter from Dr. Moment. While he, too, pointed out the difficulty of living off campus, he was enthusiastic about my coming to Goucher and said I could probably be a work-study student in his lab. In triumph, I wrote to the admissions office, included a copy of Dr. Moment's letter, and announced that I would come to campus for an interview. I think Tony paid for my plane ticket, as my summer wages had once again gone to the family.

I drove to Goucher and met Miss Flowers, the director of admissions. She was very tall and imposing and wore a hat. The hat got my attention; hats were for solemn occasions such as Easter, weddings, funerals. I didn't know that proper Baltimore ladies wore hats almost all the time. Miss Flowers proceeded to grill me for over three hours. She probed my spotty academic record, questioned my commitment, and made it clear that while Dr. Moment could get me an interview, she had the last word for admission. I returned to Bethesda chastened, with an assignment to write an essay explaining my spotty record and my future plans. I labored over that two-page essay, and Tony made helpful editorial comments. I sent it off, and three days later received word that I was admitted, but as a junior, not as a senior. Shortly after I arrived, Miss Flowers became a good friend and a strong advocate. She later told me that she knew I had the IQ, but needed to see if I had the "I do."

I was the only off-campus student who was not living at home. I lived first across the street in a room rented from another proper Baltimore widow. The next two years, I lived in a rented room in a house owned by an old couple, Mr. and Mrs. Smith. My housemates were from Towson State College. One worked the last shift at Kentucky Fried Chicken, and we feasted on leftover chicken several times a week. When chicken didn't materialize, Mr. Smith would gruffly offer us soup from his never-empty pot.

During the school year, I worked in Dr. Moment's lab. He studied the proteins in the cuticle of earthworms, so my job was to prepare worm cuticle samples, run starch gels to separate the proteins, and then stain the proteins. He would pore over the gels and admonish himself and me that "you must cherish your exceptions"—an important lesson for a budding scientist, for it is often the unexpected result that holds the key to understanding. He also reinforced the importance of persistence and careful attention to detail.

I wanted to have a summer job in Bethesda, so one of my Goucher professors, Helen Funk, introduced me to one of her former students, Loretta Leive, a microbiologist at the National Institutes of Health. I worked in Loretta's lab for two summers, and it was there that my desire to study molecular biology crystallized. By then, Tony and I knew that we wanted to build a life together and that, after I graduated and he completed his stint with the Public Health Service, we would be moving to Boston, where Tony would do a residency in general medicine. I began applying for graduate school, asked Loretta to be one of my references, and gave her the forms for Brandeis, Tufts, Harvard, and Boston Universities. "Where is the application to MIT?" she asked me. I explained that I had not applied to MIT because I felt my math was weak and because I probably would not get in. She looked at me sternly and said that MIT had the strongest graduate program in molecular biology in the country, and if I was serious about becoming a molecular biologist, I had to apply there. So, somewhat reluctantly, I applied. MIT was the only program to accept me, and I learned that you can't get what you don't ask for.

Tony and I were married on the same day I graduated from Goucher. Grandma Margaret, Great-Aunt Linda and her husband, Greg, my parents, four of my siblings, Tony's mother Jackie, his sister Kathy, and several friends joined us at dawn at Great Falls National Park on the Potomac River for a simple wedding ceremony.

Graduate School

Tony and I settled into a small fifth-floor walk-up apartment overlooking the Victory Gardens in Boston. Tony disappeared into the intense schedule of a medical resident, and I joined my classmates at MIT. We were a small class of nine men and four women. The graduate officer was Salvador Luria, a Nobel laureate. First-year graduate students shared an office, where we kept a pet rabbit and gathered after classes to discuss phage genetics, biochemistry, the latest hot paper, or the latest seminar. The classes were demanding, and we were treated like junior colleagues in an exciting and important endeavor. I felt that I had arrived in graduate school heaven.

All students were required to take a set of courses and pass a preliminary exam before we chose a lab for thesis work. After the rigorous first preliminary exam, we got together as a class and proposed a modification for the second part of the qualifying exam. The faculty accepted our proposal to spend three days in an MIT-owned cabin in the New Hampshire woods with a couple of faculty members, giving one another seminars on topics we would research in advance. When it came time to choose a lab, we negotiated among ourselves before we approached the faculty. We discussed our budding interests, faculty personalities, lab ambience, and our ambitions. We worked out any competition for the same lab in advance and maximized the chance that all of us would be successful. I had planned to study developmental biology but did not feel that any of the developmental biology labs were a good fit for me, so I decided to study virology, as it appeared to be the best model for understanding the control of gene expression. I approached David Baltimore, an associate professor whose lab was studying poliovirus, vesicular stomatitis virus, and retroviruses. He was noted for having described the RNA-dependent RNA synthesis of the picornovirus RNA genome as a graduate student, and he had recently described reverse transcriptase, the enzyme that copied RNA into DNA in RNA tumor viruses. He told me he had no room for a new graduate student. I then approached Harvey Lodish, who was interested in protein synthesis. David and Harvey had postdoctoral fellows who collaborated on several projects, and they shared lab space and a secretary. I worked out an arrangement whereby I would study the translation of poliovirus RNA, and both Harvey and David would be my thesis advisors. I was the first graduate student in biology at MIT to have joint thesis advisors.

The first task I was given in the lab was to isolate encephalomyocarditis (EMC) virus and its RNA. EMC is a picornovirus whose RNA had been used in cell-free translation systems. The plan was to isolate EMC RNA and repeat experiments described in the literature as a prelude to preparing poliovirus RNA and examining its translation in cell extracts from various sources. David gave me a recipe he had used for isolating poliovirus, and said that since the two viruses were so similar, the recipe should work for EMC. The procedure involved growing the virus in cells, breaking the cells, and centrifuging the cell extract through a gradient of sucrose containing the detergent SDS. The detergent would solubilize the cellular proteins, but the virions would stay intact and form a nice peak that could be detected with a recording spectrophotometer and collected. I dutifully infected cells, learned how to measure the amount of virus I obtained in the infected cells, and ran a sucrose gradient—no peak. I repeated the procedure, carefully checking each reagent and checking each step—still no peak. I reported my failure to David. He made several suggestions, all of which assumed that I had made a mistake somewhere along the way. More repeats, still no peak. I finally suggested, diffidently, that perhaps EMC virus, unlike poliovirus, was dissolved by SDS. This suggestion was rejected out of hand on the basis of the similarity between the two viruses. I decided that I had not made a mistake, because by then I had successfully isolated poliovirus. So, without telling David or anyone else in the lab, I substituted a milder detergent in the sucrose gradients and successfully isolated EMC virus. I reported this minor success with a matter-of-fact manner that belied my jubilation and amazement. I was right! My incredibly successful advisor, who everyone knew would win a Nobel Prize one day, was wrong! This was an important lesson in the conduct of science. The best answers always come from experiments, and no one knows everything.

I came to love the intensity of life in a world-class lab. I learned to hold my own in lab meetings, where every experiment was scrutinized and criticized. The hours were long, the competition was intense, and the collaborations were worldwide. I became an expert in the preparation and use of cell-free protein synthesis systems. One paper I wrote was a collaboration with a group from Duke University, and another was a collaboration with investigators from the University of Naples and Washington University. When I wrote and defended my thesis in January of 1975, four papers based on my work had been published. By the time the fifth and sixth papers appeared in the literature, I was hard at work as a postdoctoral fellow in the laboratory of Fotis Kafatos at the Harvard University Biolabs on Divinity Avenue.

Success through Failure

When I started looking for a postdoctoral position, I had two goals: I had to stay in Boston, and I wanted to apply my knowledge to developmental biology. I read the literature and attended seminars. I did not seek the advice or help of Harvey or David. When I told them I was going to Fotis's lab, each was angry because they thought I had gone to the other for help. I learned that good mentors expect to be involved in such decisions.

Fotis's group used the silk moth as a model to study gene expression during the development of the silk moth eggshell, called the chorion. In the silk moth, the eggs are connected by a string of cells, and each egg is about four hours further developed than the one before it. The chorion is a beautiful structure, made of many proteins that are synthesized in a developmentally regulated manner. I was awarded a prestigious Helen Hay Whitney postdoctoral fellowship to support my work in Fotis's lab. I planned to apply my knowledge of protein synthesis to the study of the chorion proteins.

Two years after I began postdoctoral work, I had accomplished very little despite lots of hard work. My only publication was a non-peer-reviewed symposium paper in which I was listed as a middle author. Since productivity as a postdoc, as measured by peer-reviewed papers, is essential to getting a good job, I was anxious and depressed. These feelings were exacerbated because important work was going on all around me and all over the country. My lab mate, Argiris Efstratiadis (whom we called Arg), was collaborating with Tom Maniatis to show that reverse transcriptase could be used to make DNA copies of messenger RNA. Wally Gilbert's lab, two floors up, was developing chemical sequencing of DNA. Molecular cloning techniques had been developed and used to isolate eukaryotic genes. Genes encoding proteins were turning out to be interrupted by long stretches of DNA whose function was unknown. I began to feel that my successes as a graduate student were accidental. Since translation of the chorion RNAs did not seem to be a viable strategy for understanding their regulation, I began the process of trying to isolate their genes using the scientific grapevine to learn about and apply the latest unpublished techniques for cloning DNA. During this time, cloning genes became a heated political issue as well as the most exciting science around. Cambridge, always a hotbed of political activity, banned the use of recombinant DNA in the city. As a result, Tom accepted an invitation from Jim Watson to continue his work at the Cold Spring Harbor Laboratory in New York. Arg continued the biochemistry in Fotis's lab, and I went with Tom to continue the attempt to clone silk moth eggshell genes. I grumbled that there had been many migrant farmworkers in my family, but I was the first migrant postdoc.

Everyone who worked at Cold Spring Harbor (CSH) had to isolate and characterize a restriction enzyme to help build the catalog of available enzymes for use in recombinant DNA technology. I was assigned the task of characterizing the restriction enzymes in *Bacillus globigii* (Bgl) and, as far as I know, was the first person to separate Bgl I from Bgl II and determine the best salt conditions for their activity. Such work was considered a necessary part of teamwork and was never published. The exchange of enzymes was a routine event; Arg and I later made a very large batch of Hinf from *Haemophilus influenzae* and traded it with Rich Roberts for small aliquots of every enzyme in the CSH refrigerators. Rich was an investigator at CSH who had undertaken a systematic search for restriction enzymes as a means of generating small fragments of DNA. He later won a Nobel Prize for the discovery of discontinuous genes.

In the meantime, I prepared silk moth DNA, cut it with various restriction enzymes, and attempted to attach it to a bacterial plasmid. The combined DNA, in a solution of calcium, was mixed with a preparation of *E. coli* strain Chi 1776, a strain of *E. coli* deliberately debilitated by gene deletions and mutations, and the only strain of bacteria that could be used to clone genes from insects and mammals. It was a long and complex series of procedures that took many days. The last day of preparation was a long one, and I'd spread my bacteria on a plate of agar and wearily walk down the dark road to my dorm room. I'd be up early the next morning to examine my plates, but week after week, nothing grew. In retrospect, this is not at all surprising; we were using the wrong tools under suboptimal conditions. It was as if I had tried to reshape Cold Spring Harbor Bay with a shovel and a pick. *E. coli* 1776 died in large numbers under the conditions required to force DNA through the membrane, genomic DNA could not be efficiently connected to plasmid DNA, and the plasmid I was using did not replicate well. Tom Maniatis later developed an elegant means of using phage to efficiently clone large genomes, perhaps in part inspired by my failures.

Almost one year after I had arrived at CSH, I piled my clothes, bedding, petri plates, and small equipment in a corner of a large rented truck, the only size available, and drove back to Boston. I had been home only a few times that year, reluctant to stop my weary routine, always thinking that maybe this time it would work. Tony had visited me at CSH once and had spent most of his time in the library while I worked. I didn't have any results, but I knew what didn't work, and I knew a lot about some of the critical steps in cloning. The most valuable thing in the seventeen-foot truck was an ice chest with tubes of enzymes; one tube in particular contained terminal transferase, a small aliquot of the only preparation in the United States that worked reliably.

Back at Harvard, I used these enzymes and my hard-earned knowledge to clone human globin cDNAs prepared by Arg, using material provided by colleagues at Yale. This work gave me a peer-reviewed paper, but I was still a middle author. I was contemplating beginning a job search when Arg approached me with the proposal that I join him in a project he was doing with Wally Gilbert to clone insulin cDNA. That began a six-month period that was one of the most exciting scientific periods of my life and resulted in a paper and a patent. The paper, describing the production of insulin in bacteria, assured my scientific reputation. The patent opened a door into the business side of science and awakened my interest in the intersection of science with business and law.

The cloning and expression of insulin was the start of my career as an independent scientist. I declined Wally Gilbert's invitation to join Biogen, the company he founded as we were immersed in the insulin project, and accepted a position at the University of Massachusetts Medical School. I did agree to be a consultant to Biogen, and one month after starting my job, I took a monthlong leave of absence to go to England to try to clone and express human insulin, an attempt that failed. The story of the race to produce insulin using recombinant DNA is described wonderfully in *Invisible Frontiers* by Stephen Hall.

A Life in Science

As a new assistant professor, a woman, and a minority, I soon found myself serving on many university committees. I also took on a heavier teaching load than might be expected at a medical school, and was on more thesis and advisory committees than any other faculty member in the department. As a result, my scientific productivity in those first crucial years was low, and when I came up for tenure, it was a battle. Susan Leeman, a professor in physiology and an eminent scientist who had discovered and characterized substance P, took me under her wing during that difficult time and provided essential advice and support. I was granted tenure and left one year later for a nontenured position at Children's Hospital in Boston and Harvard Medical School. The tenure process had been a painful lesson in setting priorities, and I decided that it might be easier to keep priorities straight in the more explicitly demanding setting of Harvard. While the move was a good one for me, the reason for moving was not. The measures of good science are the same in any setting, and I knew it. Like so many others, I had not understood the unwritten rules of advancement, and I had said yes to committees and teaching and students and had left too little time for the science.

By the time I established my lab at Children's Hospital, molecular biology had become more of a tool than a field, and rather than focusing on a single biological problem, the members of my lab and our collaborators used molecular techniques to explore interesting problems in cell biology, endocrinology, and neuroscience. We made substantive contributions in several areas, and my students and fellows went on to establish their own labs. Over time, it became increasingly difficult to support the broad scope of studies I found most satisfying. I felt that I had to either devote myself to one problem or seek another way of maintaining an involvement in a broad array of scientific areas. I spent several months talking to colleagues and mentors, friends and family. It was Eleanor Shore, a physician who was the dean of faculty affairs at the medical school, who helped me realize that I could make a contribution by using my administrative skills. By then, I was deeply involved in the graduate program at Harvard Medical School, I had served as acting chair of the Division of Neuroscience during a turbu-lent time in the division's history, and I was an active member of the governance committees at Children's Hospital. I called Alice Huang, a microbiologist who had left her lab at Children's Hospital to become a dean of science at New York University, to ask her about such a transition. I began to look into administrative jobs and got a call from Auerbach Associates, a search firm looking for an associate vice presi-dent of research administration for Northwestern University. While the job sounded intriguing, it was in Illinois, and so I told the caller I could not move. A couple of days later, I got a call from the head of the firm, Judith Auerbach, who said, "If you are interested in a job like this one, you should look at it, you don't have to take it." So I went to Evanston and met Bill Kern, the vice president for research and a theoretical chemist, and spent the day talking to faculty. I returned to Boston excited by the possibility, but the fact that it was in Illinois seemed insurmountable. Tony and I talked about the commute and what it would entail, and we worried about the separation. Tony's sister Kathy pointed out, dryly, that we both worked so much, we probably would see each other more. We decided to try commuting, and so we did, for seven years.

There is more to the story, of course. I have more to do and more to say. A life in science is not necessarily easy, but then neither is life itself. A life in science has been a way for me to embrace life, with all its challenges and demands.

APPENDIX

Latinas in Science, Technology, Engineering, and Mathematics

Deborah Santiago
Vice President for Policy and Research

*L*atina representation in higher education has changed. In 1976, Latinas represented 45 percent of Latinos in higher education. In 2004, 59 percent of all Latinos enrolled in higher education were female. (National Center for Education Statistics 2005).

In 2004, one-third of Latina freshmen surveyed at all four-year colleges intended to major in science and engineering fields; this percentage has not changed since at least 1983 (UCLA Higher Education Research Institute 2005).

While Latinas enroll in college in greater numbers than Latinos, men greatly outnumber women in engineering programs. In 2005, Latina undergraduates represented 22 percent of Hispanics enrolled in engineering programs (Engineering Workforce Commission 2005).

Degrees Earned

Latinas earned 60 percent of all bachelor's degrees awarded to Hispanics in 2005, but only 37 percent of degrees in science, technology, engineering, and mathematics (STEM) (National Center for Education Statistics 2005, table 262).

Latinas earned more than half of the bachelor's degrees awarded to Hispanics in biological and biomedical sciences (63 percent), and almost half (46 percent) in mathematics. However, women received 24 percent of bachelor's degrees awarded in engineering, 27 percent in computer sciences, and 43 percent in physical sciences (National Center for Education Statistics 2005, table 262).

Latinas lag behind males in degrees earned in all STEM fields except biology and sciences. In 2003–04, 70 percent of associate's degrees, 63 percent of bachelor's degrees, 52 percent of master's degrees, and 54 percent of PhDs awarded in this field to Hispanics were earned by Latinas (National Center for Education Statistics 2005, tables 259, 262, 265, 268).

The top five institutions awarding degrees to Latinas in biology in 2003–04 were in Puerto Rico (2) and Texas (3). The top two institutions were the University of Puerto Rico, Mayagüez (138), and the University of Texas, San Antonio (98) (National Center for Education Statistics 2006a).

The top five institutions awarding degrees to Latinas in mathematics and statistics in 2003–04 were in Texas (3) and California (2). The top two institutions were the University of Texas, Brownsville (18), and the University of California, Los Angeles (14) (National Center for Education Statistics 2006a).

Workforce

In 2003, Latinas represented 1 percent of employed scientists and engineers. The majority of these Latina scientists and engineers (60 percent) had a bachelor's degree as their highest degree earned (National Science Foundation 2006).

Latina STEM faculty has the largest representation in biological sciences. In contrast, Latino STEM faculty have the largest representation in mathematics and computer sciences (National Center for Education Statistics 2006b, table 233).

In 2003, 11 percent of Latina PhDs in science and engineering who were employed at colleges and universities were professors. Just over 15 percent were associate professors, and 37 percent were assistant professors. In comparison, 30 percent of Latino PhDs in science and engineering were professors, 20 percent were associate professors, and 23 percent were assistant professors (National Science Foundation 2006, table H-25).

Works Cited

Engineering Workforce Commission. 2005. *Engineering and Technology Enrollments, Fall 2005.* Washington DC: American Association of Engineering Societies.
National Center for Education Statistics. 2005. *Analysis of Integrated Postsecondary Education Data System, Enrollment Survey, Fall 2004.* Washington DC: U.S. Department of Education.
——. 2006a. *Analysis of Integrated Postsecondary Education Data System, Completions Survey, 2004–2005.* Washington DC: U.S. Department of Education.
——. 2006b. *Digest of Education Statistics, 2005.* Washington DC: U.S. Department of Education.
National Science Foundation. 2006. *Science and Engineering Indicators, 2006.* Washington DC: National Science Foundation.
UCLA Higher Education Research Institute. 2005. "Survey of the American Freshman." Available at www.gseis.ucla.edu/heri/cirpoverview.php.

Contributors

Norma E. Cantú currently serves as a professor of English and U.S. Latina/o literatures at the University of Texas, San Antonio. She received her PhD in English from the University of Nebraska, Lincoln. She is the editor of a book series, Rio Grande/Rio Bravo: Borderlands Culture and Tradition, published by Texas A&M University Press. Her publications include numerous scholarly articles about the border, Chicana literature, and folklore. Author of the award-winning *Canícula: Snapshots of a Girlhood en la Frontera* and coeditor of *Chicana Traditions: Continuity and Change* and *Telling to Live: Latina Feminist Testimonios,* she is currently working on a novel tentatively titled *Champú, or Hair Matters*, and *Matachines de la Santa Cruz*, an ethnography of a religious dance drama from Laredo, Texas.

Elma González is professor emeritus in the Department of Ecology and Evolutionary Biology at the University of California, Los Angeles. She received her PhD in cellular biology from Rutgers University, New Brunswick, New Jersey, in 1972. Her research interests were focused on mechanisms and roles of biomineralization in the marine phytoplankton. She has been a member of several professional scientific societies. She is one of the founding members of the Society for the Advancement of Chicanos and Native Americans in Science (SACNAS) and is currently an elected member of its board of directors. She has published over fifty articles in peer-reviewed scientific journals and books. She received research funding from the National Science Foundation, the National Instititues of Health, and the Office of Naval Research from 1976 to 2002. She has had a long-standing commitment to educational issues relating to minority student access to careers in science, mathematics, and engineering as a MARC program director at UCLA and as a member of review committees at the National Institutes of Health, the National Science Foundation, and the College Board. She was recently a member of the advisory committee of the UCLA Chicano Studies Research Center, and a former member of the editorial board of *Aztlán: A Journal of Chicano Studies.* In 1998 Dr. González was honored by the College of Letters and Science at UCLA through the establishment of the Elma González Award for Distinguished Undergraduate Research. Dr. González received the Outstanding Scientist Award from SACNAS in 2004, a Pioneer Women Award from Los Angeles Commission on the Status of Women in 2005, and the Distinguished Teaching Award from the Academic Senate at UCLA in 2005.

Aída Hurtado received her doctoral degree in social psychology from the University of Michigan. She was born and raised in south Texas. Currently, she is a professor of psychology at the University of California, Santa Cruz. Author of a number of articles, her books include *Voicing Chicana Feminisms: Young Women Speak Out on Sexuality and Identity, The Color of Privilege: Three Blasphemies on Race and Feminism,* and the coedited *Chicana Feminisms: A Critical Reader.*

Diana Marinez is an emeritus professor and dean of the College of Science and Technology at Texas A&M University–Corpus Christi and an emeritus professor of biochemistry and molecular biology at Michigan State University. Dr. Marinez has published in journals such as the *Journal of Agricultural and Food Chemistry* and the *Journal of Dairy Science.* Throughout her career, she has also had an interest in research that explores the factors affecting Latinos' participation in science and mathematics. Prior to coming to Texas A&M University, Corpus Christi, she held various positions at Michigan State University. She was the chairperson for the department of natural science and education program director for the Julian Samora Research Institute. Dr. Marinez was born in Laredo, Texas, and received her BA in chemistry from Incarnate Word College in San Antonio, Texas, and her doctorate from Indiana University Medical Center, majoring in biochemistry. During her career, she has been a consultant for scientific organizations and agencies such as the National Academy of Sciences, the W. K. Kellogg Foundation, the National Institutes of Health, and the National Science Foundation. She has received the Hispanic Educator of the Year Award from the Michigan State Board of Education, and the Distinguished Faculty Award for Excellence in Teaching at Michigan State University. She is the recipient of the 2007 SACNAS Distinguished Professional Mentor Award. Dr. Marinez is married, has two married daughters, and is a proud grandmother to Maya.

Cleopatria Martínez is professor of mathematics and has also served as chair of the department of mathematics at Phoenix College, one of the ten colleges of the Maricopa County Community Colleges District in Phoenix, Arizona. She was a tenured instructor in the Denver public schools (four years), at the Denver Auraria Community College (ten years), and at Scottsdale Community College (ten years). She received her BA in mathematics from the University of Denver and both her master's and doctoral degrees from the University of Colorado, Boulder, in education and in bilingual mathematics education, respectively. She has served on review committees for the National Science Foundation and the National Institutes of Health, and she demonstrates her commitment to education through membership in various organizations and attendance at conferences, including the Society for the

Advancement of Chicanos and Native Americans in Science, the Arizona Association of Chicanos for Higher Education, the National Conference of La Raza, and the National Conference on Race and Ethnicity in American Higher Education. She continues to work for equity in education for all people, and especially for people of color. Dr. Martínez is a single parent with three grown daughters and a fifteen-year-old son.

Lupita D. Montoya is an assistant professor of environmental engineering at Rensselaer Polytechnic Institute, in Troy, New York. She received a BS in engineering (applied mechanics) from California State University, Northridge. She holds an MS in mechanical engineering (thermosciences) and a PhD in environmental engineering (indoor air quality and bioaerosols), both from Stanford University. She received postdoctoral fellowships and training from The State University of New York, Albany, and from the Harvard School of Public Health. Her main area of expertise is aerosol science, with a particular focus on biological aerosols. Her research interests lie at the intersection of engineering and health. She studies various aerosols and how they may affect a physiological response, particularly regarding respiratory conditions such as asthma. She is also involved in the development of exposure assessment tools to identify the links between exposure to air pollutants and health outcomes. Similarly, she develops instrumentation and techniques to measure and control aerosols, including allergens, nanoparticles, and others, all of which are important to homeland security. Through her teaching, Dr. Montoya creatively merges the use of technology and social responsibility to improve engineering education and the promotion of sustainable development. Dr. Montoya's work has been funded by the Environmental Protection Agency, the National Science Foundation, the National Institutes of Health, and the National Collegiate Inventors and Innovators Alliance.

Elvia Elisa Niebla is the former national coordinator for the U.S. Department of Agriculture Forest Service Global Change Research Program. As a working scientist, Niebla did basic research on the attenuation of pollutants by soil, and has published in scientific journals such as *Water, Air and Soil Pollution* and *Soil Science*. Prior to accepting the appointment with the Forest Service, Dr. Niebla worked for the Environmental Protection Agency (EPA) and the National Park Service. For her work at the EPA, she was awarded one of its highest honors, the Bronze Medal for meritorious work. She received her doctorate in soil chemistry from the University of Arizona. She has been a senior executive fellow at the John F. Kennedy School of Government at Harvard University, attended the Senior Executive Institute in Charlottesville, Virginia, and has been a Brookings Fellow on Capitol Hill.

Elizabeth Rodríguez-Johnson graduated from New Mexico State University with a BS in 1975, an MS in 1976, and a PhD in 1980. She began her civil service career as a mathematician at the Pacific Missile Test Center. Currently, she is a senior policy analyst with the Developmental Test and Evaluation/Systems Engineering Office within the defense systems directorate of the Office of the Undersecretary of Defense for Acquisition, Technology and Logistics (AT&L). In this capacity, Dr. Rodríguez-Johnson develops and institutionalizes policies and practices that enhance the awareness and importance of good systems engineering within the Office of the Secretary of Defense. Previously, she was the deputy director for the Department of Defense's interoperability. From 1998 to 2000, Dr. Rodríguez-Johnson was the director of the AT&L Y2K Management Office, exercising responsibility for seven functional areas: logistics, weapons systems procurement, environmental security, science and engineering, facilities and installations, and nuclear, chemical, and biological. Her government service has included assignments with the director of defense research and engineering, Department of Transportation, the White House Office of Science and Technology Policy, the Department of Defense director of operational test and evaluation, the Naval Research Laboratory, the House of Representatives, and the Office of Management and Budget.

Elsa Cantú Ruíz received her doctorate in curriculum and instruction, with an emphasis on mathematics education, from Texas A&M University, College Station. She received her BS in elementary education with a major in mathematics from Texas A&I University at Laredo, and her master's degree in secondary education from Laredo State University. She also holds a State Board of Education Mid-Management Administrator Certificate from Texas A&M International. After twenty-seven years as a middle school and high school mathematics teacher, she became an administrator and assumed the duties of coordinator of the K–12 mathematics program for the Laredo Independent School District. She also served as the testing coordinator for the district and as an assistant principal. Currently, she is an assistant professor of mathematics education at the University of Texas, San Antonio. Her research interests include mathematics education in the 6–12 curriculum and, more specifically, the motivation of Latina/o students in mathematics classes. She has been an active member in the Society for the Advancement of Chicanos and Native Americans in Science, the National Council of Teachers of Mathematics, and Kappa Delta Pi.

Deborah Santiago received her doctorate from the University of Southern California in education policy and is the vice president for policy and research at *Excelencia* in Education, a nonprofit organization that focuses on Latino student success in higher education. She brings her extensive experience in education policy and research to the challenge of accelerating Latino student success. Dr. Santiago has degrees in economics, urban affairs, and education policy.

Lydia Villa-Komaroff received a PhD in cell biology in 1975. During her professional life, she has held research positions at Harvard University, the University of Massachusetts Medical Center, Cold Spring Harbor Laboratory, Children's Hospital in Boston, and Cytonome, Inc. In 1996, she moved to full-time administration; from 1998 to 2003, she was vice president for research at Northwestern University in Illinois, and from 2003 to 2005 she served as vice president for research and chief operating officer of the Whitehead Institute in Cambridge. In 2003, she was appointed to the board of directors of Transkaryotic Therapies, Inc., a biopharmaceutical company that develops products for the treatment of rare diseases. She became chair of the board in January 2005, and guided the deliberations and process that led to the sale of the company for $1.6B. She joined Cytonome, Inc. as chief scientific officer in 2005 and became chief executive officer in 2006. She is a member of the Hispanic Engineer National Achievement Hall of Fame, and a fellow of the Association for Women in Science. She has served on review committees for the National Institutes of Health and National Science Foundation. She has been a member of and served as an officer in a number of committees and boards, including the Institute of Medicine Committee on Assessing the System for Protecting Human Research Subjects, the National Research Council Committee on the Organizational Structure of the National Institutes of Health, the congressionally mandated National Science Foundation Committee on Equal Opportunity in Science and Engineering, as well as the National Science Foundation Advisory Committee for the Biology Directorate, which she chaired from 1997 to 1998. She also served on the National Advisory Neurological Disorders and Stroke Council from 2000 to 2004, and was elected to the board of directors of the American Association for the Advancement of Science in 2001. She is a founding member of the Society for the Advancement of Chicanos and Native Americans in Science, and has been both a board member and vice president of the organization. She became chair of the board of trustees for Pine Manor College in May 2007.

María Elena Zavala is a graduate of Pomona College and the University of California, Berkeley. She has worked at the U.S. Department of Agriculture, Yale University, and Michigan State University. Currently, she is a professor of biology at California State University, Northridge. She has spent most of her career studying plant development, particularly roots. She was the first scientist to show the distribution of a plant hormone, cytokinin, in roots. She has published the results of her work on plants in various scientific journals. Her research efforts have been funded by the Ford Foundation, the National Science Foundation, the U.S. Department of Agriculture, and the National Institutes of Health. In addition to her interests in plants, she is interested in educational equity issues, has worked to develop science curricula for K–12 teachers, and has established and directed programs that seek to increase the number of minorities in the sciences. She has also worked on projects that seek to increase the participation of women in science (American Women in Science, Women in Science and Engineering, and Women in Cell Biology). She has served on the National Institutes of Health advisory boards, and has reviewed proposals for the National Science Foundation, the National Institutes of Health, and the U.S. Department of Agriculture. She was the first Chicana president of the Society for the Advancement of Chicanos and Native Americans in Science, the premier minority scientific organization in the United States, and has been recognized by the California State University system for her success in mentoring students. She is a recipient of the Presidential Award of Excellence for Science, Mathematics, and Engineering Mentoring, awarded to her by President William Jefferson Clinton.

Martha Cecilia Zúñiga received her BA in zoology from the University of Texas, Austin, and her MPhil and PhD in biology from Yale University. She received postdoctoral training at the Yale University School of Medicine and the California Institute of Technology. She has held faculty appointments at the University of Texas, Austin, and at the University of California, Santa Cruz. Her PhD training was in nucleic acid structure and function, but throughout most of her career, she has focused on the cell biology and function of major histocompatibility complex (MHC) molecules and on viral mechanisms that interfere with MHC function. As a professor of molecular, cellular, and developmental biology at the University of California, Santa Cruz, she currently conducts research on the development of T lymphocytes and mechanisms of immunological tolerance. The National Science Foundation, the National Institutes of Health, and the California Cancer Research Coordinating Committee have funded her research, which has led to both primary research articles and invited review articles. In 1989, she was awarded the Presidential Young Investigator Award. In 2000, she was featured at the Tech Museum of Innovation in San Jose, California. She has served on the minority affairs committee of the American Society for Cell Biology, on the advisory committee of the National Institutes of Health RIMI Program at Texas A&M University, Kingsville, on predoctoral fellowship review committees for the Ford Foundation and the Howard Hughes Medical Institute, and on the postdoctoral fellowship review committee for the California division of the American

Cancer Society. She has reviewed research grants for the National Science Foundation, the National Institutes of Health, and the U.S. Department of Agriculture. She is a past member of the policy committee of the California Cancer Research Coordinating Committee, and a present member of the advisory committee for the UC LEADS undergraduate research program. She is a lifetime member of the Society for the Advancement of Chicanos and Native Americans in Science. Her service to this organization includes membership on its board from 1989 to 1995 and the reviewing of its poster abstracts for many years.